mastering the
toltec way

A Daily Guide to Happiness, Freedom, and Joy

Dr. Susan Gregg

Red Wheel
Boston, MA / York Beach, ME

First published in 2003 by
Red Wheel/Weiser, LLC
York Beach, ME
With offices at:
368 Congress Street
Boston, MA 02210
www.redwheelweiser.com

Library of Congress Cataloging-in-Publication Data

Gregg, Susan,
    Mastering the Toltec way : a daily guide to happiness, freedom, and joy /
    Susan Gregg.
        p. cm.
    Includes bibliographical references and indexes.
    ISBN 1-59003-050-8
    1. Conduct of life. 2. Toltec philosophy—Miscellanea. I. Title.
    BJ1595.G76 2003
    299'.792—dc21

                              2003013947

Typeset in Truesdell
Printed in Canada
TCP
10 09 08 07 06 05 04 03
 8 7 6 5 4 3 2 1

To the magic of the moment and the love that lives there

contents

acknowledgments

The list of people that made this book possible is immense. I am so grateful to everyone who has ever touched my life, especially the difficult ones. Without each of them I wouldn't be who I am. I am very grateful that Sister Sarita so freely offered me her love, that don Miguel Ruiz asked me to be his student, and that I said yes.

I humbly thank all my students, those who were and are part of my life. You have taught me much. I thank Bea for her love, patience, and endless edits. My animals' unconditional love has filled my heart and enriched my life.

This list would be incomplete without my parents; my agent, Sheree Bykofsky; Janet Rosen; Amanda Pisanni; and my editor, Robyn Heisey, who all shared my vision. And of course I thank the universe for rainbows.

introduction

The Toltec people, mighty warriors and conquerors, introduced war to Mesoamerica. When they encountered the knowledge of a race I have come to call "the ancient ones," they embraced it and made it their own. A secret society dedicated to preserving this ancient wisdom developed within the Toltec civilization. In response to being conquered by the Spanish, the secret society took that knowledge underground, where it was passed on in secret from master to apprentice for hundreds of years.

The knowledge embraced by the Toltecs transcends normal, everyday awareness. It offers a way of life that is expansive, freeing, and joyful. You can learn how to be happy no matter what your life holds and have the complete freedom to be yourself.

I was fortunate enough to meet Sister Sarita when she first began to openly share her knowledge. She and her son, don Miguel Ruiz, became my teachers, and I studied with them for many years until I completed my apprenticeship and was told to go and teach in my own way. I am grateful to be able to share with you the gifts the knowledge of the ancient ones has brought to my life.

The ancient ones knew that life, as we perceive it, is an illusion. They knew that "reason's" perception of reality was just a point of view, and a limiting one at that. Our minds don't understand that we are part of an expanding, loving, living, and intelligent universe. As we begin to identify our true nature, we can align ourselves with the spirit instead of the mind. Shifting the source of our personal power from the mind to the spirit allows us to release our limited thinking and embrace our limitless nature.

In the Toltec tradition, there are three masteries: the mastery of awareness, the mastery of transformation, and the mastery of intent. They overlap and weave together to form a beautiful tapestry. Awareness allows you to change the way you look at the world. Transformation is rich with tools that will assist you in changing your life in a profound manner. Intent will teach you how to focus your attention on what you do want instead of what you don't want. As you learn to apply these masteries to your life, magic will happen.

The Grandmother is the personification of the feminine aspect of the ancient ones' timeless wisdom. Let her stories speak to your heart and your soul. The stories, meditations, and exercises offered here will help you break free from your old, limiting way of viewing the world. The life of freedom you are creating will require you to leave your mind behind. This book will help you do just that.

The Stories

The ancient wisdom was an oral tradition. The stories presented here are part of that tradition. Read them and let them work their magic in your life. Perhaps you'll discover one that so speaks to you, you will feel called to read it over and over. Perhaps the stories you like the least will have the most to teach you.

Stories teach us in ways often not clear to us. Let the ancient ones speak to your heart and your mind. Write your own stories, and include yourself in them. What part would you play? Become part of the stories and allow them to become part of you.

The Toltecs realized there were two distinct ways to view the world: first attention and second attention. In first attention we focus on the world our mind sees. And in second attention we become aware of the world our spirit perceives. These stories will speak to you on both levels.

The Moon

It takes the moon twenty-eight days to complete a cycle, and each year we have thirteen moon cycles. This text follows the moon's pattern. I suggest you start this book on the full or new moon and use it every day.

There is something magical about standing in the light of the moon. When the idea for this book was growing in my heart, my students and I performed a full moon ceremony on the North Shore of Oahu. We were standing on the beach and I had just finished telling a story. When I turned with my hand pointing skyward, there before me was the full arch of the most beautiful rainbow I had ever seen. Before that, I had thought night rainbows were only part of Hawaiian mythology.

The moon causes the tides to rise and fall. It is only natural that our bodies are affected by its cycles as well. Start to observe the moon as it moves through the sky. Pay attention to its cycles. Do you notice any relationship between your energy levels and the moon's phase? Get an appointment book that includes the moon's cycles. Each day write down a few short notes about how you felt that day emotionally, spiritually, and physically. Take note of any major events in your life. You can look back later to trace any patterns.

The Meditations

Scattered throughout the text you will find brief visualization exercises. Allow yourself to enter into these meditations as fully as possible. Set aside ten or fifteen minutes when you won't be disturbed, and get as comfortable as possible. Take a few deep breaths to relax your mind and your body. If any part of your body feels tense, breathe relaxation into that tense area.

Focus your attention on your breathing. Then, starting either at your head or your feet, contract and release each of your muscle groups. After you feel completely relaxed, read the meditation and think about the images it presents. Allow yourself to become part of the meditation. Step into it and fully embrace the experience. It is easier than you think. Use your imagination, play with the images, and enjoy the process.

Try this one right now: Imagine yourself picking up a beautiful, juicy lemon. Cut it in half, hold it up to your nose, and savor its fresh smell. Now take a big bite of the lemon. If you let yourself really think about that lemon, you probably found yourself salivating. Guided meditations are really games of "let's play pretend."

Repeat the meditations as often as you wish. You can also record them or have a friend read them to you. You may want to keep notes of your experiences and notice how they change over time.

The Exercises

You can join a gym, but if you never go to it, your body will stay the same. If you go to the gym, hang around talking with people, do a minimal amount of exercise, your body may change a little. But if you go to the gym and really work your muscles, your body will get strong and fit.

So it is with these exercises. You can buy this book and seldom look at it, or you can dedicate a year to really doing the exercises and transforming your life. Just thinking about these exercises will do very little for you. They are designed to assist you in having a deep and abiding connection with the essence of who and what you are. Do these exercises passionately, with all your heart, an open mind, and all your soul. You are worth the effort.

Be gentle and loving with yourself and praise yourself for your courage and effort even if you don't think you are doing it perfectly.

Much of this process is experiential. I remember the day don Miguel told me that he had taught me all he knew and it was time for me to go and teach in my own way. I thought he was crazy. He explained that most of the information I had was still unavailable to my conscious mind, that I had learned it in altered states, in dreams, or in meditations. My job would be to build my personal power so I could remember it.

These exercises will lead you gently through the process of disengaging your mind and re-engaging your spirit. Many of them may not make sense; you may not "feel" anything while you are doing them, and you may not enjoy some of them. You may want to just read them. But *do* the exercises, don't just read and think about them—actually do them. Do them more than once, and make sure you do the ones to which you put up the most resistance.

You may want to keep a journal of your experiences. You may want to do the exercises with a group of friends. Keep doing the exercises until your life changes. Experiment, play, resist, rant and rave, laugh, cry, but keep doing the exercises.

My hope for you is that you will abandon yourself to this process. Let the magic of this ancient wisdom fill your heart and your mind. Let go of all of your limiting beliefs, agreements, and assumptions; remember that your limitations exist only between your ears.

The exercises and meditations presented here are tools, and as with any tool, they can be used to hurt or to heal, so always be gentle and loving with yourself as you use them. I kicked and screamed all the way, but even though it went against my nature, I didn't listen to my mind. I showed up every day for years. When I first started studying with Sister Sarita and don Miguel, neither one of them spoke any English and I spoke no Spanish. For the first year and a half that I studied, I had no idea what I was studying, I just knew I needed to be there with them. I listened to my heart and not my mind.

Read the stories, do the meditations and exercises, use the tools, and surrender to the love that surrounds you always.

With love,

Susan

The Grandmother's Gift to Us All

All night the Grandmother stood staring at the horizon, softly chanting and praying to the Great Spirit. Deep purples and swirls of orange heralded the coming dawn. The wind stirred restlessly and caressed the embers from last night's fire, turning them bright red. A few feet away a rabbit sat watching while an owl circled overhead, moving effortlessly over the land.

As the gentle glow of the new day flowed over the land, the Grandmother sat down at the edge of the cliff. Her prayers had been answered. She remembered the first time she had sat on this cliff, at the beginning of her new life.

The Grandmother had spent her life connecting with her divinity and power, teaching others how to heal themselves and hear their own quiet, still voices. Now her days upon the earth were done. She was ready. She welcomed death and breathed easier; the Great Spirit had shown her how to leave behind the gifts so freely given to her. She wanted others to see their own beauty, to feel the love that surrounds them, to live their lives joyously and with ease. She wanted all human beings to know how to leave their limitations behind.

As a young girl she had failed to heal the great Chief and had been banished from her village. She had forgotten that it was the Great Spirit that healed through her. Even though it was the Chief's time to die, she had believed it was her failure. She'd listened to her fears and doubts. She knew she had done something wrong. If only her heart had been purer or she'd prayed harder or used different herbs.

Eventually she stopped loving herself and lost all contact with the Great Spirit. She wandered the land aimlessly, lost in her private torment. The people she met were kind, but she wouldn't allow herself to feel their love. She would stay in a place for a short time, teach the children with her stories, and heal their sick. Then she always moved on.

A wound deep in her soul stopped her from feeling happy. She had cut herself off. Her heart ached. Sickness, disease, and death all seemed like a cruel joke. She could not open her heart and allow herself to love others, only to have them die. Then the love would be gone again. During this time, many fine men courted her, but she never opened her heart to any of them. She wouldn't take the risk.

One day, as she crossed the desert, Father Snake came to her. He rattled loudly at her, but lost in thought, she never heard his warning. She had almost stepped on him when his fangs sank into her leg, slowly spreading his powerful medicine into her veins. He looked at her sadly as he slithered noiselessly away. He could see the pain in her heart. His medicine, the medicine of creation, was very powerful. It would either kill her or help her to remember her connection with the Great Spirit.

The Grandmother took refuge in a cave and for many days she was lost in fever. She had become very ill by the time an old woman came to her and placed herbs on the wound, gently lifted her head, and wiped away her tears. The old woman fed her nourishing broth and sang songs of love and kindness to her. As the Grandmother slowly began to heal, the old woman asked her if she was ready to hear the truth.

Nodding weakly, the Grandmother listened as the old woman began. She told of the ancient earth mysteries, she taught how to harness the thunder beings and call the spirits of the land. The old woman showed her how to make the four directions—north, south, east, and west—her friends and guardians. She talked about the love of self, about faith and joy and happiness. The old woman shared with her all the teachings of the ancient ones.

As the Grandmother listened, tears of gratitude filled her eyes. At last she heard the words for which her heart had longed. She drank in the knowledge and felt love fill her heart for the first time in years. How she loved that old woman.

After the fever broke, the Grandmother looked for the old woman, but she had gone. As the Grandmother arose her step was light, and she could feel the life in everything around her. The world was full of love, and she laughed at the foolishness of her old ways. The rocks and the plants talked to her. The plants showed her how each generation fed the next with their love.

The animals showed her how life and death were just a magnificent dance. They told her the secrets of their powers, and she opened her heart to their love. For the first time in years she felt truly alive and at peace. Father Snake came and rejoiced with the others. He was so glad she had chosen to heal her heart rather than die. She thanked him and told him she would give thanks every day that her spirit had been set free.

She climbed to the top of the great mountain and sat in prayer for a day and a night. In the morning her prayers were answered and she knew what must be done. She had always had the gift of physical healing, but now she also knew how to heal the human heart—a far greater gift.

The Grandmother left that place with a deep love for herself, for others, and for life itself. She came to a great village that stood at a crossroads, a center for trade that many traveled through. In the village she clearly saw how the belief that we are separate from each other and from the Great Spirit caused all of life's suffering. Now that she viewed life through the eyes of love, she clearly saw everyone as part of the great mystery. No one is ever really alone.

The people of the village were touched by her love and her wisdom and asked her to stay. Because the Grandmother knew it was her destiny to teach many, she made the village her home. For many years she taught the young with her stories, and her gift as a storyteller brought many to her village. Children came from all over to sit at her feet, to study, and to learn. Many a great healer and chief had learned the ways of the Great Spirit through her stories.

chapter 1

By the Light of the Moon

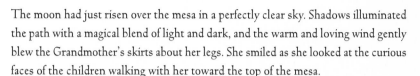

The moon had just risen over the mesa in a perfectly clear sky. Shadows illuminated the path with a magical blend of light and dark, and the warm and loving wind gently blew the Grandmother's skirts about her legs. She smiled as she looked at the curious faces of the children walking with her toward the top of the mesa.

She felt so blessed; her stories had taught so many generations about the sacred nature of life and the great mysteries. Silently she said a prayer of thanks to the Earth Mother.

Then the Grandmother broke her silence. "As you walk upon the land always make sure to give thanks. With each step you take you leave a little bit of yourself behind. Do you want to leave love or fear in your footsteps?

"The earth is alive. She knows you by your touch. She knows your heart. When you open yourself to the magic of nature, all things become possible."

The wind stirred, and off in the distance an owl spoke. "What did you just hear?"

The youngest girl replied, "I heard the wind as it caressed the land and Grandfather Owl greeted it with his song. I heard love."

The Grandmother was pleased. She nodded and walked on. The rocky trail grew increasingly steep. "Let the rocks speak to you. They will guide your feet and make your passage easy. Trust, quiet your mind, and allow yourself to feel the power in the earth."

When they reached the top of the mesa, each took a place in the circle of sacred stones. A fire already burning sent sparks leaping into the night sky. The Grandmother began her story.

"Look around, my children. Let yourselves feel the love and the magic in the light of the moon. Open your hearts and let the moon love you. Breathe deeply and feel.

"Light is light, yet notice how different the light of the moon is from the light of the sun. Look down at our village and see how the land about it sparkles. Feel the magic in the air. Sit in the light of the moon and let it embrace you; look into your heart and see what you feel."

Off in the distance a coyote howled. "The moon is constantly changing. We measure the seasons with her passage. She reminds us of the nature of life. Each month her light goes out and the night sky darkens, filled only with the stars. Then slowly the moon grows until it once again fully illuminates the evening sky.

"If you watch the moon each night, you will learn much. We are spirits; we are energy, and the moon will show us how to align ourselves with that energy. The moon will help us connect with our divine nature.

"Sit under the night sky each evening and let yourself feel. Quiet your mind and feel the presence of the Great Spirit. Breathe and let the moon teach you with her love, her wisdom, her gentleness, and her strength.

"Notice where the moon rises and where she sets. Each day, notice where the moon is in her cycle and what your relationship is to the world about you. Allow yourself to feel the energies as they flow through you. Become aware of yourself as you go through your own inner journey. Take the time to let the moon teach you."

The Grandmother stood, and her voice blended with the wind. She called upon the four directions, asking them for protection, wisdom, and strength. Next she called upon the Great Earth Mother. She called forth the spirits of the ancestors, the ancient ones, the spirits of the land, and the Great Spirit of all things great and small. Once she felt the power of the moment surround her, she invited the children to offer up their prayers and to ask the moon to teach them. The magic of the night embraced them, and the children learned many lessons that night by the light of the moon.

day 1

What Do You Expect?

Expectations can be incredibly powerful tools for bringing about transformation or for creating disappointment. There are many different types of expectations: negotiated and un-negotiated expectations, conscious and unconscious expectations.

What do you expect to gain by reading this book? Do you expect your life to magically change without any effort on your part? Do you expect change to be hard and require a great deal of work or to be easy and enjoyable?

Do you expect that if you only had _____ (a better job, a lover, more money—you fill in the blank) your life would be fine? What do you expect of your friends? Do you expect them to take care of your needs so you don't have to set boundaries? Do you expect everyone to like you and make choices based on your desire to be liked?

What do you expect from yourself? What do you expect from life? Take some time and become aware of your expectations in relationship to improving the quality of your life. I know that if you do these exercises daily and continue to apply the principles set forth here for a year, your life will change dramatically.

If you really expect magic and miracles to occur in your life, they will. You can have a life free of limitations once you let go of the expectations that limit you.

Once you become aware of old, limiting expectations, you can change them by repeating your new expectations ten or fifteen times a day for at least a month. Every time you notice an old expectation, observe it, remind yourself you are letting it go, and then—with as much passion as you can muster—repeat your new expectation.

DAY 2

Contract with Yourself

Affirm your dedication to fully engaging with this book by writing a contract with yourself. Put down exactly what you wish to do or gain in relationship to these exercises and your spiritual explorations. Include the statement that you will abide by your contract, then sign it, date it, and put it someplace where you will see it daily. Do this now and enforce your contract with yourself. As the Grandmother advised, "Become aware of yourself as you go through your own inner journey."

Day 3

Personal Freedom

Freedom allows us to choose how we "walk upon the land." But the definition of our personal freedom is more intimate. Define what personal freedom means to you. How will you feel when you achieve it? What will your life look like? What will you do during the course of a typical day?

My own definition of personal freedom has transformed over the years. At first my definition focused on external circumstances—a great job, a nice place to live, a loving relationship, and the ability to create whatever I wanted. It evolved into the ability to make all of my choices based in love. I thought I had finished redefining my personal freedom, then one day I realized my definition had become "maintaining a deep and abiding connection with my spiritual self."

Write down your definition of personal freedom and be sure to revisit that definition frequently. Take note of how it evolves.

DAY 4

Meditation

We tend to make meditating much harder than it really is. There are hundreds of ways to meditate, and none is inherently right or wrong. You can meditate with your eyes open or closed. You can repeat a mantra or a phrase or a prayer. You can focus on an object while sitting, standing, walking, in nature, at home, in a church, or anywhere else for that matter. You have not failed if you can't quiet your mind. Follow the advice of the Grandmother and "Open your hearts and let the moon love you. Breathe deeply and feel."

The easiest way to begin a meditation is by focusing your attention on your breathing. Take several slow, deep breaths, and notice your breath. How does it feel? Where do you feel it in your body? Follow your breath as it effortlessly flows in and out.

If you find your mind wandering, bring your attention back to your breath. The Grandmother chose the mesa in the moonlight, but perhaps a different image works better for you. For instance, imagine yourself standing at a train station. Trains come and go. You can stand and watch them go by or get on and go for a ride. Think of your thoughts as trains. As soon as you find yourself lost in thought, get off the train and go back to focusing your attention on your breath.

Practice, gentleness, and love will make meditating much easier and more enjoyable. Over time your meditations will grow and change, just as you will. Avoid comparing yourself or your experiences to anyone else.

Day 5

Habits and Routines

The Toltec tradition is really a method of retraining your mind so you can create your reality from your spirit. One way to begin this retraining is to experiment with breaking old habits and routines. "The moon is constantly changing." Even cycles and routines change. Try some of the following:

- Go to work a new way.
- If you're usually on time, be late; if you're often late, be early.
- If you're a vegetarian, eat meat; if you're a meat eater, don't.
- Change the way you dress—try bright colors instead of muted colors or flowing skirts instead of tailored pants.
- Wear shoes that don't match.
- Comb your hair with a different part or style or don't comb it at all.
- If you meditate every day, stop; if you don't, begin to.

Decide to change your habits and routines for a full week. Notice how often you remember to change them and how often you just slip back into old habits.

Which do you want to be in charge of your life—your mind or your spirit?

Day 6

Moon Journal

"If you watch the moon each night, you will learn much," the Grandmother said.

Get a small calendar, preferably one that shows the moon's cycles. On it, write a few words about each day. You could simply take note of what you did or how you felt—a sort of "internal" weather check. Note whether your emotional climate is stormy or sunny with light breezes.

After you have kept the journal for some time, go back and read through it. Do you notice any patterns between your "internal" weather and the cycles of the moon?

Day 7

Moonbeams: A Meditation

Let the moonbeams transport you to another time and place. "When you open yourself to the magic of nature," the Grandmother said, "all things become possible." Imagine standing in the middle of the desert surrounded by a group of loving friends. Ancient chants fill the air. The full moon shines over the mesa. The wind begins to stir. You bow your head and move your feet rhythmically to the sounds around you in a dance you've never been taught.

The ancient chants fill your heart and your mind. Feelings stir deep within your being. You feel your connection to everyone and everything. Breathe in the love around you, and let the ancient chants and dances take you. Surrender completely to the magic of the moment.

day 8

Filter System

Fear is an illusion. We live in a safe, limitless, and totally loving universe, yet we experience lack and limitations. Our fears stop us from seeing the richness life has to offer. Fear is False Evidence Appearing Real. Our filter system clouds the true, loving essence of everything and everyone.

Our filters tell us many lies—that we need to be right in order to be happy, that we must protect ourselves, that intimacy is something to crave and fear simultaneously. Without knowing it, we stop seeing the richness life has to offer and instead think our filter system represents reality.

Today, pause as you move through your day, look around, and ask yourself: How could I see this differently? How would this look if I saw it through the eyes of love?

In the words of the Grandmother, "Sit in the light of the moon and let it embrace you; look into your heart and see what you feel."

DAY 9

There Is No "Out There"

This thing we call reality is totally subjective—it depends on what we tell ourselves at any given moment. Reality or "out there" is not real at all; it is just a projection of the story of our own lives. Our filter system distorts our perception of reality and then we react to that distortion. But the external universe is neutral.

Today pretend there is no "out there." If you find yourself upset by someone or something, remind yourself that there is no "out there." If you don't like how you are feeling, simply tell yourself a different story.

Day 10

Dominion and Domination

Learning to see life from the perspective of dominion instead of domination was a long journey but the most rewarding one I have ever taken. In dominion you see everything through the eyes of love and acceptance. You learn how to embrace all of life, even the most challenging parts.

Today carry around a piece of paper, divided into two columns. At the top of one column put the word *loving*, and at the top of the other put the word *judgmental*. Whenever you find yourself having a loving or judgmental thought, put a check mark in the appropriate column.

Set your intent to observe life and yourself from a place of dominion. Notice how it feels when you put checks in the loving column instead of the judgmental one. Do you judge even that?

Love even your judgments. As much as possible, practice embracing all of life. "As you walk upon the land always make sure to give thanks."

DAY II

Acting

We are all actors on a stage. You are the actor, director, scriptwriter, and projectionist of the movie of your life. You can rewrite the roles anytime you wish. "Each day," said the Grandmother, "notice where the moon is in her cycle and what your relationship is to the world about you."

Decide on a role to play today. Pick something completely different from the role you usually play, or choose the role you often play that you like the most.

DAY 12

Meeting Your Spiritual Essence: A Meditation

The night is very dark and cold. You've been walking on this lonely road for a long, long time. Off in the distance you see the light of a flickering candle. You keep walking; the light remains, off in the distance, but it seems no closer. You grow weary. You want to sleep, but to sleep surely means death. In the silence of your heart, you ask for help.

You close your eyes for an instant and when you open them again you find yourself in a magnificent temple filled with light. Standing in front of you is a beautiful being of light who reaches out and touches your head and your heart. You become one with the being and see yourself as you really are. You are one with your perfection. You are one with your divinity, and you breathe a huge sigh of relief. You're home.

Day 13

Awareness

Awareness is the first of the three Toltec masteries. Our awareness of ourselves and of life has many levels. We can see everything as an opportunity to redefine ourselves in either a more expansive or more limiting way—we influence that choice by what we tell ourselves. Being aware of that can be quite a challenge because we take things personally.

A useful awareness exercise is to simply observe your mind. Observe your thoughts until you can see them as opinions. Notice your thoughts and then ask yourself whether each opinion is expansive or limiting. How are you aware that you are aware? Where does your awareness come from? What awareness do you use to answer these questions?

DAY 14

Emotional Neutrality

Life is totally emotionally neutral. Life is as it is, and then we have an opinion about it. "We are energy," the Grandmother explained, "and the moon will show us how to align ourselves with that energy."

We generate any emotional response we have to an event by what we tell ourselves about it. No one, no event, absolutely nothing can *make* us upset or happy; we generate our emotions internally. Once we start to have an emotion, it is too late not to have it. If that thought "makes you" angry, feel the emotion, let the energy flow through you, and then notice what you told yourself that generated the emotion. Today, begin to explore how your opinions affect your emotions. Experiment with changing your opinion and see what happens to your emotions.

DAY 15

Clouds

When I was a little girl, my mom and I would watch the clouds and make up stories about the images we saw. We imagined lots of unicorns, horses, whales, fish, the occasional giant, elves, and angels waving.

We often get so caught up in our minds that we forget to enjoy the beauty and wonder of the physical universe. Take some time today and lie on your back, look up at the sky, and just watch the clouds. They float aimlessly about, never resisting, never judging, always fluid and free. What can the clouds teach you?

DAY 16

Energy of Gentleness

When I am harsh and critical, I feel very small and weak. The more critical I become the more powerless I feel. When I am loving, gentle, and understanding, I feel expansive and strong.

The Grandmother advised, "Breathe and let the moon teach you with her love, her wisdom, her gentleness, and her strength."

Today, play with the energy of gentleness. Can you find the strength that lies within it?

DAY 17

Daily Routine

What can you do every day to assist you in creating the life of your dreams? Write? Pray? Meditate? You could spend time in nature, exercise, read, use the tools scattered throughout this book, do breathing exercises.

When I lived by the beach, I watched the sun rise while I wrote, did some stretching and breathing exercises, and then meditated while listening to the waves.

Create a daily routine that works for you. Experiment with it and remain flexible; allow your routine to grow and change with you.

day 18

Energy States

In the Toltec tradition the universe is viewed as a vast energy system. Energy is either expanding or contracting, never stagnant. It is always in motion.

We each have our "favorite" energy state, one that feels safe and familiar. It may even be a state we profess not to like, such as anger or sadness, or a role we'd rather not play, such as victim.

Discover your favorite energy state by noticing the one you find yourself in most often. Allow for the possibility that it is an energy state, that it isn't based on external events. Just observe without judgment—unless judgment is one of your favorite energy states! By observing, you can begin to learn how to change an energy state whenever you wish.

DAY 19

Ethereal Energy

We are made up of physical, spiritual, and ethereal energy. The latter is what we access when we enter an altered state of consciousness called second attention, where we become aware of the world our spirit perceives.

Our ethereal body allows the spirit to exist in physical reality. Ethereal energy vibrates at a higher frequency. "The earth is alive," the Grandmother reminds us. "She knows you by your touch."

Take a deep breath and let yourself feel your ethereal body. What do you imagine it looks like? Imagine that energy feeding your life force. Be patient with yourself; it takes time to be able to actually feel these energies.

DAY 20

The Grandmother: A Meditation

You walk through the forest and the trees are so thick that the sun barely reaches the ground. The path, covered with moss, feels soft underfoot. Filled with a deep sense of gratitude and love, you are going to meet the Grandmother. You have known her for years. She lives in your heart, and she speaks to your soul. You walk a little faster. You can't wait to see her again. You've heard her stories since you were a young child.

The path leaves the forest and takes you through a field of tall grasses. Off in the distance you can see a village. As you approach children come out to greet you, laughing and offering you cold clear water. You drink and feel refreshed. You are expected. They lead you to your room and give you a meal. Although you are eager to see the Grandmother, you wait patiently. The sun begins to set, and you follow the children.

You round the corner and there she is, smiling at you. She puts out her hand and motions for you to sit beside her. You look into her eyes; in that instant you know she has always been with you. She is the love that lives deep within your being. You sit beside her, allowing yourself to be filled with her presence, and you give thanks.

Day 21

Discipline and Dedication

Discipline and *dedication* are two words I used to hate. But once I changed my attitude about these concepts, I found that if I applied a little of each to my life, miracles began to occur.

What images do those words conjure up for you? Are your definitions of the words expansive or limiting? How can you apply discipline and dedication to the exercises in this book? How can you use discipline and dedication to improve the quality of your life?

DAY 22

Recapitulation

Recapitulation is a way of using intent and the breath to release energy trapped in the past. Emotions are energy in motion; when we see the present through our filter system, that emotional energy doesn't flow freely. Old emotions can actually change our experience of the present moment.

Recapitulation releases such energy. In recapitulation there are two types of breaths—mindful inhalation and mindful exhalation. Use inhalation to recover the energy you have attached to anyone or anything external. Use exhalation to help you release another's energy that you have taken in, such as anger or judgment.

To use the breath of inhalation to recapitulate, breathe in as if you are sucking through a straw. Exhale normally. Continue to inhale mindfully and exhale normally until you feel finished.

To use the breath of exhalation, blow out as if you are extinguishing a candle. Inhale normally and place the emphasis on exhalation until you feel a sense of release.

Always explore an issue with both types of breaths in one sitting. You may have to repeat the process several times before you really feel finished. When you have let go of an issue, you will have a sense of clarity and know how your belief structure created the issue.

Day 23

Transformation

Transformation is the second of the Toltec masteries. Many of the exercises we have done so far provide us with the tools to transform. We can use these tools to separate our emotions from our actions and literally transform limitations into doorways to our limitless nature.

In order to transform something we must first become aware of it. The awareness that all events in life are emotionally neutral allows us to use our emotional responses as stepping stones to personal freedom. Our emotions become guideposts, leading us to our limiting beliefs, agreements, and assumptions.

Recapitulate an event, track a behavior until you understand the beliefs behind it, write until you can't write anymore, meditate, go to your power spot, do anything that assists you in transforming the energy state you are in.

Today, utilize one of the tools of transformation. Take action until your perspective changes.

DAY 24

Procrastination

The path to happiness requires us to take action. Too often we spend more time thinking about getting something done than it would actually take to do it. The following exercise helped me overcome procrastination.

Each day make a list of three things that you will accomplish before the end of the day. Always set yourself up for success. For example, don't write "clean the house"; break it down into doable tasks. Be realistic: Write "clean the bathroom" and "organize my desk." Make this a habit so that after a while you know that if you put something on the list, you will get it done.

Day 25

The Edge of Time: A Meditation

The wind roars, lightning strikes all around you, and rain pelts down. The storm seems to be getting stronger. You stand at the opening of the cave and feel a shiver run through your body. Moving toward the rear of the cave, you sit down against the back wall. As lightning illuminates the interior, the ancient symbols covering the walls seem to come alive. You find yourself being pulled into the void where the darkness swirls around you.

You are suddenly walking noiselessly down a corridor. The floor and the ceiling move closer together. You stand before a small door at the end of the corridor and, looking back, you can see the turbulent storm in the distance.

You open the door and time stands still. You stand at the edge of eternity and realize that everything exists in that moment. You feel yourself everywhere and nowhere. Standing at the edge of time, you look at the world with new eyes.

27

Day 26

Intent

Intent is the third Toltec mastery. It is very powerful and always operating in your world. Intent is like the wind; you can see its effect—as when the wind moves a sailboat—but you can't see it directly. Although it is always working, you must set your intent clearly in order to use it. The Grandmother said, "Let the rocks speak to you; they will guide your feet and make your passage easy."

If you look at your life, you can see your intent. If you are unhappy, your intent has been to create unhappiness. If you have a loving relationship, your intent was to have a loving relationship. To see your intent simply look at the results you have achieved in your life.

You can harness intent just as you can harness the wind. I've been learning how to sail a small catamaran, which has been a great lesson on intent. Small adjustments make a big difference. I can set my intent to go toward a certain spot, but I need to pay attention and adjust the rudder and the sail along the way or I won't get there.

Set your intent to achieve personal freedom. You may discover that everything but freedom will come roaring to the surface. Welcome the arrival of each new belief, make an adjustment or two, and set your intent again. See what comes up, address it, and keep repeating the process until you get to where you want to go.

Be gentle with yourself in the process. Be grateful for the limitations your intent shows you rather than judging yourself for having them.

DAY 27

Energy

Physicists have found that when an atom is split into sufficiently small pieces, the pieces will act like waves if the observer believes in wave theory and will act like particles if the observer believes in particle theory. The energy of the universe is aware of the beliefs of the observer.

But are we observers aware of the energy? Hold your hands about three inches apart and focus your attention on the area between your hands. Slowly move your hands closer together and farther apart. Concentrate on your hands and notice what you feel. Give yourself permission to experience the area between your hands. Relax, breathe, and feel.

Today, focus your attention on feeling the energy of your life force through your hands. Take time to practice feeling the variety of energies that always surround you. Touch different objects and notice their energies. What does a plant's energy feel like? An animal's? A chair's?

Day 28

A Practice

This path is not just a collection of exercises, nor is it merely a philosophy. It is a way of life, a way of being in this world that is expansive and engenders joy. I think of it as a practice that takes daily practice.

Imagine if all the food you were going to eat in your lifetime were placed in front of you and you had to eat it immediately. The thought of doing so would be overwhelming. But when you eat one meal at a time, you can easily accomplish the task. Learning how to live with passion, joy, and freedom may seem unrealistic. The idea of being happy no matter what is happening in your life may even seem insane at times, yet with a little bit of practice it can become a reality.

This path is a practice. Do a little each day and see what happens to the quality of your life. Practice with all your heart, your mind, and your spirit.

chapter 2

Seeing

"I see what you mean," said the young boy.

"I don't think you do," the Grandmother replied. "You see only your own desires and forget about the desires of others."

The young boy was the son of a great chief, but true leadership requires more than blood. The boy seemed unable to see the world through the eyes of love. His eyes were blinded by thoughts of power. The Grandmother knew teaching this boy to really see would be a great challenge.

"Follow me," she said.

Anger flashed in the young boy's eyes, but the Grandmother silenced him with a look. She turned and walked away from the village. The boy had a hard time keeping up with the Grandmother. The longer they walked, the angrier he got. *Who does she think she is to treat me this way?* he thought. *I am the son of a chief, and I deserve respect.*

"You deserve nothing, little one," said the Grandmother. "Respect is something you must earn by being loving and treating others with respect."

The boy wondered how she knew his thoughts. After several hours of walking they came to a place few had seen, a place very sacred to the Grandmother.

"Sit and be with the stillness," the Grandmother said as she sat down in the clearing with her back to the young boy and stared at the horizon. As the sun slowly sank into the valley, the land turned pink then orange then deep purple. Night fell and coyotes howled. The young boy felt afraid. As the Grandmother moved into the darkness, she prayed the spirits of the land would touch his heart. The boy tried to follow her but his legs wouldn't move. He was cold and hungry and his mind was full of fear.

As he sat and stared at the path before him, he began to see small lights. Everything began to shimmer and glow. He felt warmth fill his heart and spread throughout his entire being. He remembered his mother's gentle touch before she died, and he wept. His anger and sadness poured out of him. He felt someone touch his arm and looked up, expecting to see the Grandmother; instead he saw a wolf. Although the boy's heart raced in fear, the wolf merely stood, looking deeply into his eyes. To the boy's amazement he saw love there—for the first time in his life, he saw the true spirit of love.

He spent the night wandering, touching the plants, talking to the animals, and thanking the Great Spirit. At dawn he went back into the clearing. The smell of corn bread and venison greeted him. The Grandmother smiled as he approached. He saw her spirit and fell at her feet. She lovingly stroked his head and began to talk to the boy about the power of love and the power of spirit. She spoke of being of service and of giving to others.

He looked up at the Grandmother, smiling broadly, and said, "I see what you mean."

The Grandmother nodded and replied, "I think you do." And his training began.

Day 29

Embracing Everything

Imagine taking someone you really care about into your arms and embracing
her lovingly. Imagine holding her close to your heart, being filled with
tenderness and joy. Now imagine being able to feel that way about everything
in your life, even your biggest petty tyrant. If you could do that, how would
your life change? What beliefs would you have to change in order to feel
that way? "The boy seemed unable to see the world through the eyes of
love. His eyes were blinded by thoughts of power."

Today allow for the possibility that you can embrace every moment of
your day. Observe how you stop yourself from doing that.

Day 30

Being in the Moment

When we are fully present in the moment, concepts like fear fall away. Fear pulls us out of the moment. If someone pointed a gun at you, *in that moment* you would have nothing to fear. You would be afraid of an event that might happen in the future—that this person would pull the trigger. And if that happened, you would be afraid of getting hit by the bullet. But notice that fear is always about an event occurring outside of the present moment.

When the boy dropped his anger at the Grandmother, abandoned his thoughts of his future greatness, and let go of his fear of the dark woods, he could be in the moment with the creatures of the forest.

Focus your attention on the moment, notice your thoughts, observe your emotions, and then explore what energy you feel in your body. Whatever you discover embrace it, accept it, love it, and then let it go. Holding on to anything stops us from being in the present moment. Practice being here now, letting that now go, and being here now, and in the next moment, and in the next.

DAY 31

Loving: A Meditation

Imagine yourself sitting next to a radiator on a cold day. It gives off heat. Allow yourself to bask in its warmth. Notice how the heat flows to everything around it.

Now imagine you are the radiator. Feel the warmth flowing out of you with ease. Now imagine that heat becoming love, radiating to everything around you. Imagine yourself just loving.

DAY 32

Balance

Balance is a very important element. Without balance it is impossible to achieve integration. When we fall out of balance, it's almost impossible to remain connected with ourselves and our spirit.

Do you do something every day to balance your spiritual, emotional, and physical being? If not, make a specific plan to nourish all sides of yourself every day; follow through with your plan.

DAY 33

Thoughts or Emotions

Some of us get caught in our thoughts, while some of us get caught in our emotions. If you have a hard time experiencing your emotions, you need to connect with your emotional side. If you tend to be very emotional, you need to connect more with your thought process.

To separate our emotions from our thoughts, we need to be able to fully access both. Do you tend to think about your emotions? Practice feeling your emotions rather than talking about them. Or do you allow your emotions to think for you? Practice talking about what is going on from an intellectual standpoint.

Do this with the intent of achieving a balance of thoughts and emotions. Once we achieve balance, it is easier to choose how to act rather than react to the events in our lives.

DAY 34

Personal Importance

A society based on domination nurtures personal importance, which is very seductive. It is part of the illusion and assists us in maintaining our version of reality. *Who does she think she is to treat me this way?* the boy wondered about the Grandmother. *I am the son of a chief, and I deserve respect.*

When we give in to personal importance we disconnect from our spiritual self. We focus our attention on what we can't control or easily change—the externals—and fail to focus internally on what we can change, our filter system.

As you move through the day, notice where you focus your attention. Notice how it feels when you give in to personal importance. How does it feel when you focus on "out there"? How does your body feel? Do you want to be right or be happy? What emotions are dominant? Does your energy feel expansive or is it contracting?

DAY 35

A Day in the Life

Spend the entire day as a homeless person. Observe how you feel and how other people treat you. If you have been homeless before, go back to your old haunts and see how they feel now.

Ask people for money. Go without a few meals. Stay out until after dark, then go home, and write about your experience. How does your life look now?

Perspective, as the chief's son discovered after a night alone in the woods, can give you a new outlook.

Day 36

Making Things Non-Negotiable

We never negotiate our need for air. We never put off our next breath until tomorrow. If we want to continue to live, breathing is non-negotiable.

When I first started studying the Toltec tradition, I had a white index card in the corner of my bathroom mirror with a list of four non-negotiable things. I remember getting out of my warm bed many nights to finish that list.

I was fortunate to realize early in my studies that action is the key to change. I watched people talk about how much they wanted to change, yet their lives remained the same. On the other hand I watched other lives blossom and grow. I observed that some people took consistent action while others didn't.

Insights, knowledge, and profound experiences will do little to change your life if you don't take different actions. As long as you put star-shaped ice cube trays in the freezer, you will always have star-shaped ice cubes. Our thoughts, beliefs, agreements, and assumptions are energy patterns. As long as we hold onto them, we will continue to get the results we have always gotten.

What four things—if you did them every day—would make the most difference in your life? My list is (1) write, (2) meditate, (3) look in the mirror twice a day and tell myself how wonderful I am (and believe it), and (4) go to the beach to connect with my divinity.

Do you want your life to be full of happiness and joy or pain and struggle? The choice is yours. It depends on how willing you are to make a few things non-negotiable and do them every day.

Day 37

Action

Awareness alone won't change anything. Unless we take action nothing will change. Today, experiment with a new action. Take the day off, run through the house naked, dance wildly, do something completely out of character, and have fun while doing it. Recall what a simple thing like spending the night in the woods did for the chief's son.

Day 38

Magical Sailboat: A Meditation

As you walk down the dock, you see a beautiful little sailboat with a colorful, inviting sail. The boat looks very safe and somehow feels loving. You stand in front of it, take a deep breath, and step aboard.

You nestle into the fluffy pillows propped against the back of the sailboat. The rudder and the sails adjust themselves as you begin to effortlessly move toward the setting sun. A sense of peace and acceptance fills you. You're not sure of your destination, but it doesn't matter. Gulls fly overhead, the boat rocks gently, and the air tastes fresh and salty. All is well in your world.

You realize that life is like a magical sailboat. You may not be sure where you are going but you can enjoy the ride. When the chief's son surrendered himself to the dark night, he found he could touch the plants, talk with the animals, and see love in the wolf's eyes. Surrender to the peace of your spiritual self, and allow yourself to nestle into life and enjoy the ride.

Day 39

Curiosity

Curiosity is a wonderful tool. Think about how it feels—expansive and open. When you approach life with a sense of curiosity, you never really know what you will find.

When you believe you know what you are looking for, you will usually find what you expect. The energy of the statement "I know" is closed; there's no need to explore because you already "know" the answer.

Play with the energy of curiosity. Approach your day, your decisions, and your process with a sense of curiosity, and see what happens. Ask yourself, "How else could I see this? What else could I tell myself?"

DAY 40

Addictive Thinking

Today you will think 95 percent of the same thoughts you had yesterday. We tend to have the same thoughts over and over. We seem addicted to thinking and established thought patterns. Use that addiction to develop new responses and thought patterns.

Make a set of index cards with new thoughts, quotes, exercises, and pictures designed to help you retrain your mind. Read them whenever you start thinking addictively.

DAY 41

Expectations

There are many types of expectations—negotiated and un-negotiated, realistic and unrealistic, conscious and unconscious. Expectations are a very powerful force in our lives. If you expect to be abandoned, you will be. If you expect to be disappointed no matter what people do, you will be.

In relationships we often have many un-negotiated expectations. While we may not voice our expectations, we may sit silently waiting for others to fulfill them. Although we have some realistic expectations—"I expect to take care of my own wants and needs"—we also have some unrealistic ones—"I expect you to make me feel better."

Take some time today and notice your expectations. When you are upset about something, explore your expectations. You will often find the real cause of your upset when you do.

Day 42

What Shape Is Your Container?

The container you hold up to the universe will get filled no matter what its shape. If you hold up a thimble, you'll get a thimble's worth of energy. If you hold up your mind to be filled with fear, you'll receive exactly that. If you hold up your heart to be filled with unconditional love, that is what you will experience.

What shape is the container you hold up to the universe?

DAY 43

Imagination

Imagination is a powerful tool. If you fully engage your imagination, you can burn yourself with an ice cube if you believe it is a hot poker.

Imagine what your life would be like if you truly knew yourself as a limitless being. Imagine fully experiencing your personal freedom. When you felt small and limited, how did you use your imagination to reinforce that feeling? How could you use it instead to help you connect with your spiritual essence and the magnificent, limitless being you truly are?

DAY 44

Ceremony

A ceremony is any act done with intention that assists you in connecting with your divinity. It is a loving act of power that can last minutes, hours, or days. Create a simple ceremony for yourself. Decide what elements you would like to include and where you would like to have it, indoors or out.

Make it a sacred act. Mindfully collect the items you will need and prepare the space. Say a prayer, read a poem, perhaps light a candle, and then open your heart and your mind to the magic and power of ceremony. You can make it simple or complex, long or short. The most important element of any ceremony is your intent to connect with something larger than yourself—your divinity.

DAY 45

The Blessing: A Meditation

The spring water is cold and clear. People have come to it for centuries. They have gathered from all around for the blessing. You walk nervously down the moss-covered path toward the spring, feeling tentative and expectant. You notice children walking beside you in silence. They step mindfully; joy fills their faces.

As you all enter the clearing you look deeply into one another's eyes and greet each other in silence. The birds sing, the breeze gently rattles the trees, a dog barks off in the distance.

You walk toward the center of the circle where the Grandmother approaches you and nods. She steps closer to the water's edge and dips her hands into it. When she touches your forehead with the water, you feel a jolt of energy flow through your body.

You turn and look at the people gathered around you. The Grandmother raises her hands and in a voice full of love introduces you to them. Then she turns and says to you so all can hear, "Remember, you are the blessing."

Day 46

Mirrors

Have fun with this exercise. Take a hand mirror outside and walk around backward for at least an hour; use the mirror to see where you're going. If people are around, it's even more fun. Notice how you feel as they look at you like you're crazy.

Go to a park and look at the sky, the trees, and the plants. Go to a mall, walk around backward while looking into the mirror, and watch people. Try to pick things up, fix a meal, clean the house, walk on an uneven surface, or water your plants all while looking in the mirror. Do this exercise more than once. Spend an entire day walking backward around your house. Look at yourself looking at yourself in the mirror. Talk to a friend while looking into the mirror. Observe your world in this manner, and notice your feelings, emotions, reactions, thoughts, and assumptions about the whole exercise. How does the world look when viewed through a mirror?

DAY 47

Vulnerability

Our greatest strength lies in being completely vulnerable. The mind often tells us that we need to protect ourselves to remain safe and that we should avoid vulnerability. But as long as we believe we need to defend ourselves, we can never really feel safe.

Once we begin to realize that we live in a safe universe, we can stop defending ourselves. Then vulnerability becomes desirable and empowering.

When the boy looked into the eyes of the wolf, he expected to be afraid. But when he saw love, he let go of his defenses, released his anger, and shared in the universe.

How do you feel about vulnerability? Where could you practice being vulnerable today?

DAY 48

Love

Perhaps love is the process of being lead gently back into ourselves.

Love is often easier to describe than to define. When I describe love I use words like *gentle, kind, patient, soothing, nurturing, expansive, freeing, generous, big, safe, cuddly, all-encompassing*—I could go on and on. Before I released some of the emotional garbage attached to the word, I saw love as frightening, often painful, and something to avoid. I am so glad that is no longer true for me. You can define love for yourself; if your definition causes you pain, change your definition.

One of the most important decisions you can make in life is whether you will choose to believe in a safe universe or a hostile one. When I believed in a hostile universe, I felt unhappy, depressed, and fearful most of the time. When I decided to believe in a loving and safe universe, my life changed completely. I became able to experience a freedom and joy I had never thought possible. Yes, my body can be harmed or even killed, but the essence of who and what I am cannot. I now know I am a spirit within a body, but I am not my body. I am limitless, eternal, immortal, and infinite; I am free and love has become a way of living.

As with our other emotions, love is self-generated. It does not depend on another person's actions or on external events. When we act and think in love, rather than fear, life can become a glorious, fun-filled experience.

How would you like to define *love* in your life? Think of the feeling of love. You might want to start by thinking of something or someone you feel loving toward. How does that feel in your body? Is your chest relaxed or tight? How does your stomach feel? Start at your head and scan every part of your body. What is your physical response? Now practice creating that feeling of love. Practice until you can feel it easily. Once you can do that, think of someone or something you find upsetting, and then generate the feeling of love. Does this change your thoughts about the person or event?

DAY 49

Noticing Energy

What colors are on the wall behind you? What kind of energy do you feel around you? How does your energy feel? What kind of a day will this be?

Notice the energy within you and around you today. Set an hourly timer. Whenever it goes off stop for a moment to really take in your surroundings—how the energy feels around you and how you feel in relation to that energy. Notice how that awareness affects how your day progresses.

Practice choosing how you want to act instead of reacting.

Day 50

Patience

A rosebud that receives ample water, light, and warmth will, in time, open to become a beautiful flower. But if you try to hurry the process by tugging at the petals, you will only injure the flower. Are you tugging too hard on the petals of your life? Are there areas of your life that could use your patience? Where do you need to take action, and where do you need to practice patience?

Learning to live in dominion is much easier when we have a little patience with the process. What do you have the least patience with in your life? Just for today, embrace it. Maybe this will become a habit.

DAY 51

The Stars

Spend the entire night under the stars, watching the sky. Observe dawn's slow approach, and greet the sun.

How did the night feel? Did you start off, like the chief's son, in fear? Where did you end up by sunrise? Were you able to embrace the universe as safe and comforting? If not, why not? If you did, how might you carry that feeling into the day?

DαY 52

Letting the Love In

We are surrounded by a sea of love, yet we often feel alone and disconnected. Imagine yourself opening your heart and letting the love in. See love flowing into you until it fills every aspect of your being. Practice until you can really feel it.

The son of the great chief left the forest having seen the true spirit of love for the first time in his life. If you open your heart, you can too.

DAY 53

Feeling the Energy

Go to a public place, perhaps a mall, train station, airport, park, or even a schoolyard. Find a place where you can sit quietly. Close your eyes and focus your attention inside of yourself. Simply notice your feelings. Do you sense someone near you? Does it feel like an adult or child, male or female, a couple? Observe your impressions, then open your eyes and see who or what is actually there. If you want, wear sunglasses so people around you can't see whether your eyes are open or closed.

Practice until you can feel the energy of people nearby. Then build your sensitivity until you can determine their sex, age, and mood. Begin to learn the language your mind uses to speak to you about energy. We all respond to the energies around us, and as we clear up our assumptions about that energy we can learn to respond differently. Energy is simply energy until we tell ourselves a story about it.

DAY 54

The Path: A Meditation

You have been climbing steadily for hours, and the view has become more spectacular with every step. At times others walk with you. Other times you walk alone. People have helped you over some rough spots and, in turn, you have helped others. You notice this isn't the only path. Many other paths lead to the same place. You like your path but see the beauty in the others as well.

You stop to enjoy the view. Breathe deeply of the fresh air and give thanks for the beauty and wonder all around you. You feel grateful for the gift of life. As you reach the top you see mountains in every direction. Each has its own beauty, and many paths lead to the top of each one. Other people surround you on the top of your mountain; you feel loved and supported.

You look back at your path and smile. What a lovely journey it has been.

Day 55

Acting as If

I find "acting as if" very helpful. If I want to be expansive, I act as if I am expansive. I expand my heart, breathe deeply, and allow my energy to expand. If I want to be more loving, I act as if I am more loving.

Play with the idea of "acting as if" today. Act as if you have a profound connection to your innate wisdom and goodness and see what happens.

day 56

Smile

Look at yourself in the mirror and smile. Take a deep breath and look at the image smiling back at you. Make faces at yourself. Move your hands and your body. Play with the image in the mirror until you can go beyond simply seeing yourself and feel the connection. Love yourself and allow yourself to be loved.

chapter 3

Going Inside

In the cool, dark night, they huddled close to the fire. The Grandmother's gaze drifted as she began to speak.

"The longest journey you will ever take is from your head to your heart. Your mind believes the words it speaks. It tells you stories about everything, yet it seldom stops to ask if they are true. Love or fear—the mind knows mostly fear; the heart remembers love. You can train your mind to see the love, but first you must connect with your spirit and the spirits of all others.

"You must let go of the stories your mind tells you. I am a teacher and I teach through stories. What if I told you stories of fear? What if my stories distracted you and made you look only at the illusion of physical existence? That's what the words you speak to yourself do. They distract you from what is real; they stop you from being able to feel the energy all around you.

"Our best hunters can feel the energy of the animals. They can become a deer or a buffalo. The hunters walk as the animals walk; they have a sense of oneness and harmony. They don't talk to themselves or listen to their minds. Rather, they listen to the silence within.

"Close your eyes, take a deep breath, and go within. Go beyond the noise of your mind and feel your body, feel the energies about you. With your eyes closed look all around with your heart. What do you feel?"

A young boy softly said, "I feel the warmth of the fire and the peace of the night."

The Grandmother looked at him and asked, "How do you feel warmth? How do you feel peace? How do you know what you are feeling?"

Before the boy could answer, the Grandmother continued: "As soon as you talk to yourself about what you are feeling, you are no longer just feeling. Your mind can interrupt the energy and distort it. Quiet your mind and feel. Practice until you can feel the energy, then let the energy teach you. You can't fill a gourd that is already full. Empty your mind, stand in the place of creation by knowing you don't know, and let the world teach you anew."

The Grandmother became very still and stared at the fire for a long time. "Follow your breath. Breathe and feel. Your breath is your connection to your spirit. When you want to connect with the energy of the earth—breathe the earth. When you want to connect with the spirit of your friend—breathe your friend. When you want to hunt a deer—breathe the deer. See yourself breathing them in your mind's eye, and feel your breath become one with theirs."

The Grandmother turned, looked at the fire, and took a very deep breath. "Now just breathe, know that you don't know, and feel."

DAY 57

Creating an Inner Sanctuary

I think the world would be a far different place if everyone had a safe inner sanctuary—a place to feel loved, nurtured, honored, and respected, a place to access his or her innate wisdom, strength, and love.

If you felt totally loved and accepted at all times, how would your reactions to life change? Would it be easier to tolerate things "out there"—would you be able to act in love instead of reacting?

Give yourself a gift. Begin to create a sanctuary within. Meditate and find or create that place, then begin to live your life with that connection and inner knowing.

Day 58

Holding a Space: A Meditation

Imagine that you're standing in the center of an enormous blown-glass vase. The sunlight streams through its swirls of colors, and tiny air bubbles trapped in the glass shimmer in the sunlight. You walk around inside the vase fascinated by the colors and changing light. Feel the energy of the space. Surrender yourself completely to its magic and beauty.

Now imagine yourself holding a space for yourself. Fill that space with all the love, peace, safety, and joy you can grasp. Hold that space and let it grow bigger and bigger until it encompasses your entire life and those around you.

DAY 59

Feelings

What are you feeling right now? Chances are you're either unaware of how you're feeling or you'll respond with a description of your thoughts or emotions. I define feelings as the sensations we have in our body. Our thoughts and emotions can generate these feelings, but so can our awareness of the energy that surrounds us.

Today take time to notice your feelings. Avoid trying to explain them. With a sense of curiosity, just observe them. Are they generated by your thoughts or by something external? Allow yourself to become more aware of your feelings.

Day 60

Emotions

We usually attach emotions to pieces of information that have nothing to do with reality and everything to do with how we think about reality.

Emotions are simply energy in motion. They do not have the power to do anything, nor do they have the power to make us do something. No event in life has an emotion inherently attached to it. We supply emotions with our internal dialogue.

Emotions are signposts that can help us to map our inner landscape. Understanding and changing this landscape is essential if we want to improve the quality of our lives. Every piece of information or memory we store has an action component and an emotional component. Something happened in our life; we had a reaction, and we retained the memory. The next time a similar event happens, we retrieve that information, replay the emotional component, and decide how to feel and how to react.

Our emotions and our reactions are all learned behaviors. We remember the "right" emotion, and then we dance to it like a puppet on a string. Our emotions are really a result of our filter system, which holds all of our beliefs, agreements, assumptions, and expectations. When we realize our emotions are our own creations, we can use them to set ourselves free of limiting beliefs. We can use the events in our life to illuminate our filter system. Instead of focusing our attention on our emotions and trying to change events in our lives, we can instead change the way we think.

People often say things like, "You hurt my feelings," or "You really make me angry." What actually happens is someone does something, then we tell ourselves something about what happened, and those words generate our emotional response. Once we begin to have an emotion, it is too late not to have it and important to acknowledge it.

If you are angry, write a letter you never intend to send, roll up the windows in your car and yell, beat the bed with a bat; if you are sad, cry; if you are afraid, take a deep breath and allow yourself to feel the fear. After you feel the emotion, listen to what you have been telling yourself and decide what you want to experience before you choose how to act. Stop letting your emotions tell you how to act; instead, allow them to show you what you think.

Day 61

Tools

Any tool can hurt or heal. It depends upon how we use it. The tool doesn't change; it is our intent that does.

Are you using this book to nurture yourself or are you judging yourself for not doing the exercises perfectly? Are you using the exercises to change your life or to remain the same? You can move away from pain or toward pleasure. The direction may be the same, but your experience of the journey will be very different. Once I decided to move toward love instead of away from fear, my life became much more expansive.

Which way are you moving? Be gentle and loving with yourself as you explore, shift your awareness, and experiment with a new way of being in this world. Do the best you can and know that is enough. As the Grandmother said, "Now just breathe, know that you don't know, and feel."

day 62

Tracking with Writing

Tracking is a process in which you expand your awareness of an issue in your life. If you merely cut the flower off a dandelion, the weed will bloom again. But if you get to its roots, the plant will die. The issues in your life have deep roots, and tracking will help you dig them out.

Writing is one of the most powerful and versatile tools of transformation. You can write to track your thoughts, to release emotions, to dream, to pray, to imagine. In so many ways writing can assist you in setting yourself free.

To use your writing for tracking, choose something you'd really like to change. Write that thing in the middle of a piece of paper. Then describe it all over the page. Use colors, draw, scribble, write sentences, tell its story. Dig deep to find its roots. If the issue doesn't change, dig a little deeper.

Day 63

What If?

What if you realized that you really weren't willing to change just yet? What if you suddenly discovered that you want to hold onto the issue you've struggled with most of your life? What if you decided you wanted to hold onto that old, treasured behavior no matter how much pain it causes in your life?

What if every day you asked for the willingness to let go of everything and anything that holds you back? What if you told yourself the truth, even if it was scary and painful? What is the worst possible thing that could happen? Perhaps the worst thing would be that you would really change.

Just for today walk around knowing that you really don't want to change and see what happens.

Day 64

Five Things

Make a list of five things you like about yourself and five things you don't like. Now list five things you'd like to change about yourself. Chances are that you won't want to change the things you like, but explore that too!

Next make a list of five things you love about your life, five things you hate about your life, and five things you'd like to change.

Now make a list of how you can change the things on your lists. How can you learn to love the things you hate and change the things you'd like to change?

Day 65

Mirror Work

Look at yourself in a mirror. Take a few minutes, look deeply into your eyes, and really connect with yourself as you would with another person.

Talk lovingly to yourself. Speak words of encouragement. Remember you are perfect just the way you are. Feel your energy shift as you speak lovingly to yourself. Think of the advice of the Grandmother: "Practice until you can feel the energy, then let the energy teach you."

Day 66

What Is "Normal"?

People often ask me if something they have experienced or felt is normal. I think trying to define yourself or your experience as "normal" is just another way of trying to feel safe. Normal is just a subjective measurement, simply another judgment.

Today if you find yourself wondering what "normal" is, remind yourself that normal is in the eye of the beholder. Start to create your own definition, and then start to change and mold that definition until normal no longer means anything at all.

Day 67

The Luminescent Egg: A Meditation

The illusion slowly falls away. The sharp edges begin to fade, and you see waves of energy emanating from everything. The colors move hypnotically. Even the tiniest plants send out huge spikes of light, creating shimmering rainbows.

People become huge luminescent ovals, like eggs made of iridescent glass. On the surface of each egg you see fibers, rivers of energy. Thoughts and beliefs seem to be attached to the fibers. You see the energy bodies of a close friend and of someone who upset you a great deal in the past. Other than the patterns in their fibers, they look exactly the same. You realize that on an energy level, we are all beautiful, luminescent beings.

You see that the fibers interact with one another. They stop us from experiencing another's essence. Looking down at yourself, you realize you can move your fibers with your thoughts. When you feel fear, the fibers contract and become entangled. When you feel love, they unfurl like beautiful flower petals. Take a deep breath and fill your entire being with love.

day 68

Trusting the Process

Do you trust the process? Life itself is a process. We each have a unique way of looking at life. We each decide what to change and how to change it. I can guarantee that if you take action daily, become willing to let go of your limitations, and continue to explore and reinvent your beliefs about yourself and the world, you will achieve personal freedom.

Trust the process. Remember it is a process—keep going. Don't stop five minutes before the miracle.

Explore your thoughts about trusting the process.

day 69

Do You Want to Be Right or Be Happy?

Generally, we would rather be right than be happy. We are quite adept at arguing for our limitations. Our filter system was designed to help us feel safe. We looked at life, described it to the best of our abilities, and came up with our beliefs, agreements, and assumptions. Heaven help the person or event that messes with our version of reality. We hold on to those thoughts, often at the cost of our own happiness.

The next time you find yourself at odds with someone or something, ask yourself, "Do I want to be right or do I want to be happy?" Then decide how to respond. As the Grandmother teaches, "Your mind believes the words it speaks. . . . You must let go of the stories your mind tells you."

Day 70

Impeccability

Impeccability is defined as faultless, irreproachable, and unlikely to do wrong. It is a wonderful ideal. I think of being impeccable as being harmless.

How do you harm yourself? Do your thoughts, words, or deeds in any way diminish the quality of your life? Today, practice being as loving and gentle with yourself as possible. Your ability to be impeccable or harmless will grow over time and with practice. Each day, practice being harmless with your thoughts, your words, and your deeds. For instance, when your mind tells you that you aren't good enough, remind yourself that you're perfect just as you are. You don't need to judge yourself in order to change. In fact, loving yourself just the way you are makes change easier and more likely.

DAY 71

The Way Home: A Meditation

You want to go home, to that place of peace where you know only love. You take a deep breath and concentrate on the feeling of oneness with everyone and everything. As you close your eyes and relax, you find yourself standing in front of a large door. It is carved with images of animals, plants, flowers, gods, and goddesses, but you can't see a handle. You know this is the way home, but you don't know how to get in.

Step back from the door and go deep inside yourself. Connect with that inner place of knowing. Then look at the door not with your eyes but with your heart. When you lovingly place your hand on the center of the door, it gently swings open.

You step into the most beautiful place you've ever seen and know you are home at last.

DaY 72

Big Self

I use the term *big self* to describe the essence of who and what I am—my spiritual essence, my true self or Godself. I started using that term because it doesn't have a strong emotional charge. There is my big self and my small self. My big self is aligned with personal power, my small self with personal importance. My big self is expansive, love-based, and limitless.

What does your big self feel like? Imagine spending the whole day aligned with your big self. How do you think you would feel at the end of the day?

DAY 73

Outcomes

Life is as it is. We can view life as a series of outcomes. What really matters is how we choose to deal with those outcomes. I used to think life was a series of choices and outcomes. I liked to believe that I was in control, that if I made the right choices, I could guarantee the outcomes I wanted.

What if life is really a series of random events, and our choices don't affect the outcomes? We like to feel as if we're in control. We like to believe that if we are good enough and loving enough, nothing bad can happen. We can choose to act lovingly, however, even in the face of anger, fear, or loss. That choice is all the control we really have. "Empty your mind," said the Grandmother. "Stand in the place of creation by knowing you don't know, and let the world teach you anew."

Day 74

Victims and Volunteers

In life there are no victims, only volunteers. But what, you may ask, about the children who are abused every year? What about the victims of war? From the perspective of our small selves, those are tragic events; but from the level of our spirit, those events take on a very different meaning.

Here's another seemingly harsh statement to consider: One of the greatest gifts in my life was to be sexually molested as a little girl. Granted I didn't see it that way for many years. I was only eight years old. Did I volunteer? Consciously, of course not. But because of that event I eventually remembered that this is a safe universe and that the only thing that is real is love. I worked through the experience of what I'm not—a victim—and in the process reconnected with my spiritual essence. If my small self had been able to vote on being molested in order to reconnect with her spirit, I am sure her vote would have been "no way."

But because I descended into the hell created by my habitual thought patterns, consciously decided to find another path, learned how to set myself free, and then experienced the joy of freedom, my experience of my limitless nature is all the more precious to me.

Where in your life do you still feel like a victim? Do you watch the news and react emotionally to the chaos? Or can you hold a space of love and compassion as you watch other souls work their way back to experiencing what they really are? When we assume this is a safe universe, we can look at how our thoughts make us feel unsafe. We can then change our thoughts and let the world teach us anew.

DAY 75

Magic and Power

The ancient ones saw everything in the universe as either magic or power, manifested or potential energy. We are all magicians. Everything in your life was once just a thought—it really is magic that we manifest our thoughts into action and energy. The content of this book, the ability to print the book, your decision to read the book all began as mere thoughts.

"When you want to hunt a deer—breathe the deer," the Grandmother said. You are the most powerful magician in your universe. What magical feat will you perform today? What thoughts will you make manifest? What beliefs will you magically transform?

day 76

Seeing Time: A Meditation

A fascinating light show, a web of luminescence, unfolds in the valley below. You see lights everywhere, blinking rapidly on and off, their brightness surging and fading. Occasionally balls of light streak along thin, twisting, and turning filaments. The air feels totally still, and despite all the activity below, you hear nothing, total silence. You aren't sure where you are or how you got there. You watch, curious about the lights, noticing how they move and shift, and wonder what you are seeing.

The voice of an old man startles you. "You are standing at the edge of the universe where time and infinity intersect. You are watching eternity. Everything exists in this instant. Everything is interconnected. Watch and feel. Watch the lights, and let them teach you." With that he is gone.

You know he spoke the truth. You feel honored to be standing here. Take a deep breath and allow the power of this place to fill you.

DAY 77

Expansiveness

The sky is expansive. Imagine your energy expanding like the sky. Imagine yourself getting bigger and bigger. How does it feel to be expansive?

What thoughts and emotions help you to feel expansive? Breathe in the energy of expansiveness. Let it fill your being, and then look at your life. Do you see any new possibilities? This may be a great time to use the tracking exercise; write down the emotions you feel as you embrace the expansiveness of the universe and explore the impact it has on your life.

Day 78

Pictures

Collect pictures, lots and lots of pictures. Collect images of people, animals, plants, places, and words that appeal to you. Make a collage of the images and hang it on your wall.

What does the collage say about you? Do you embrace or avoid hard subjects? Do you connect with the natural world of the sky and the moon and the wild animals? What does the collage say to you? Is it showing you the path to expansiveness?

After you live with the images for a time, repeat the process. How have the images changed? Where is your path leading you?

DAY 79

Laughter

When we laugh deeply our energy expands and becomes softer and more flexible. Our hearts open and our bodies relax. Laughter is very healing. When was the last time you laughed uncontrollably? Make laughter a regular part of your life. Watch a funny movie, or read a funny book, and let laughter take over.

Laughter is a wonderful way to affect body energy. When we feel afraid or angry, our energy contracts and becomes very brittle. When our energy is brittle, it is much harder to change it or let it go.

day 80

Dreaming

Allow for the possibility that when you go to sleep tonight you will wake up to your true nature, and when you awaken in the morning you will begin to dream. Before you go to sleep tonight tell yourself you are about to wake up. As you move through your day remind yourself you are really sleeping. Do this for several days and observe what happens when you turn things upside down.

DAY 81

Connecting with Nature

Go outside for an hour and connect with nature—touch the snow, sit on the grass and watch the clouds, observe the wind in a tree or in a field, smell flowers, watch a bee, listen to a bird, stand out in the rain and let it touch you, play in the waves. Spend at least an hour with nature, feeling it, smelling it, touching it. Allow yourself to be with nature. Let nature teach you about the peace and safety of the universe.

day 82

Thinking

As soon as we begin to think about what is happening, we are no longer in
the moment experiencing life. We spend so much time thinking and too
little time just being. Instead of getting caught up in our thoughts, we can
simply lovingly notice them. Today watch your thoughts instead of thinking
them.

Sit in a place where you may have some but not a lot of distractions. As
you sit, try to clear your mind. Perhaps a woman with a bright scarf walks by
and you think about how pretty her scarf looks. Or a dog sniffs the bushes
and appears a little thin to you. You may wonder why that man is waiting for
the bus, even though the next one won't come for a half hour. Every time a
thought appears, acknowledge it, "Oh, there is a thought," and then clear your
mind again.

You may need to start by sitting in a room with almost no distractions—
your mind will still think outside the room. Lovingly acknowledge those
thoughts and go back to simply being.

Day 83

Ask Questions

How often do we really listen to the answers to the questions we ask? When you ask questions today, concentrate on fully listening to the answers. Ask people about their beliefs and their worldviews. Listen with an open heart and an open mind. Seek out people with values very different from your own and truly hear them.

Notice how it feels when someone is trying to convince you of something. Notice how it feels to listen when you think you already know the answer. What happens when, instead of listening, you are busy thinking about your reply? How does it feel to simply be curious?

Day 84

Real Choices

We are often unclear about what our choices really are. We often choose to follow old, familiar paths rather than risk something new. We are actually choosing between our old limiting thinking, and a new life based on freedom and love.

When we are in the process of changing a behavior like overeating or smoking or fearing intimacy, it helps to understand what we are really choosing between. When I quit smoking, I realized that having a single puff meant that I was resuming my habit. When I wanted just one puff, I remembered that my choice was really between freedom and a whole tractor-trailer full of cigarettes.

Before you have that extra cookie, smoke your next cigarette, put up a wall to intimacy, or stop yourself from being vulnerable, get clear about your choices. We change moment by moment, choice by choice. It's easier to risk new choices when we are clear what those choices really mean.

chapter 4

Our Magical Bodies

The women laughed and splashed one another as they swam at the foot of the waterfall. They had just finished bathing and were enjoying the freedom of feeling the fresh, cool water on their naked bodies. The Grandmother smiled broadly as she watched the women gathered together, so filled with love and joy.

As she climbed onto the warm rocks to let the sun dry her, the Grandmother said a prayer of thanks for the wonders of her body. The wind blew crimson leaves into the stream, reminding her that winter would soon arrive. Her old bones liked the warmth of summer far better than the biting winds of winter. A young woman came over, sat beside the Grandmother, and placed her hand on her own belly.

"When will my womb be full with child? I pray and make offerings. I am so sad I don't yet have young ones of my own."

"Bodies have their own wisdom, my child. If you learn to listen to your inner wisdom you will know whether your body is ready to hold a child. Learn to listen to your body rather than your mind. Your mind is full of endless thoughts and desires.

"If you go inside, you will first become aware of your thoughts; if you go a little deeper, you will notice your emotions. Your emotions are caused by the stories your mind tells you. If you go past the smokescreens of your mind, you will be able to tap into your feelings, your body's response to the energy within you and around you.

"Take a deep breath and go within. What do you sense?"

"I feel very sad Grandmother. My heart yearns for a baby. The cradleboard my husband so lovingly crafted has sat empty for many moons."

"Go deeper, little one. Go beyond your thoughts and your emotions. What do you feel in your body? Your body is your spirit's temple; sit in the temple and listen."

"I feel a tightness in my stomach and a heaviness in my back. My breasts feel tender and my face feels hot."

"Just focus on your breath, really feel your breath as it goes in and out, and listen to the rhythmic beating of your heart. Feel the spirit within you and surrender to the stillness you feel. Let go and let yourself drift in that endless sea of love. Allow your connection to your spirit to soothe you, nurture you, and fill you with peace."

The Grandmother slowly got dressed as the young woman sat transfixed. After sitting for a long while, she began to smile. She knew her womb was ready to carry a child. The cradleboard would not be empty much longer.

day 85

Shifting Gears: A Meditation

You are driving down the road on a beautiful spring day. The road winds and climbs steadily upward. Your engine strains as you climb, and you feel it shift into a lower gear. When the road levels off, the engine shifts up and quietly hums. As you drive along the car naturally changes gears as the road rises and falls. You sit back, enjoying the ride and the scenery.

Now imagine how you move through life. You monitor your energy level, adjusting it to life's twists and turns. You adjust your thinking, shift your emotions, and choose your actions. You adjust effortlessly and easily. Allow yourself to sit back and enjoy the ride and the scenery.

day 86

The Present Moment

The only point in time that really exists is the present moment. Everything else is either history or speculation. Change can only occur in the present moment. Ironically we spend very little time fully focused on the present. Our freedom exists there. We only fully exist in the moment.

Focus your intent on being more fully present. Practice being mindful of the moment in all that you do today. When you notice yourself drifting off, planning tomorrow or thinking about what you need to do later in the day, remind yourself to come back to this moment.

Day 87

Spiritual Energy

What we perceive as physical reality is billions of particles swirling around each other surrounded by empty space. Can you see spiritual energy? What is spiritual energy? Spiritual energy exists in the spaces between the particles. We are all composed of physical, spiritual, and ethereal energy. We are mind, body, and spirit. "Your body is your spirit's temple; sit in the temple and listen," advised the Grandmother.

Allow yourself to think about spiritual energy. What do you think it is? How does it affect your life? What role does it play? What are your ideas about spiritual energy?

Day 88

Healing

When we think about healing ourselves or our lives, it is easy to step into domination, which is based on the idea that one behavior is better than another, not just different. When we think of healing from the perspective of domination, we can get caught in the belief that there was something wrong in the first place. There is nothing wrong with you or with the world for that matter. Life is as it is.

When we view healing from the perspective of dominion, we simply realize there is something we'd like to change. We can either move away from pain or decide to move toward pleasure. However, when we decide to move away from pain, we will likely create new pain to move away from and remain stuck in domination.

How do you view healing? Are you moving away from pain or toward pleasure?

Day 89

Setting Yourself Free

Our beliefs are shaped by our filter system, which in turn holds us prisoner. What belief is worth your personal freedom? Observe how your mind just responded. Is that belief really worth your freedom?

Listen to your mind's chatter and ask yourself if defending your thoughts is worth your freedom. Be vigilant with your thoughts; release the limiting ones and set yourself free.

Day 90

What Do You Want?

When I ask people what they want, they often respond with a list of what they don't want. What do you want in your life? What do you want to experience more of? What would you like to change, and how would you like to change it?

Make a list of what you want and how you want your life to look. Avoid using negatives; that just sets up negative thinking. If I say, "Don't think about something," you will immediately think about it. Focus instead on what you wish to experience. What *do* you want?

DAY 91

Love or Fear: A Meditation

Imagine the energy of love entering your entire being. Feel your heart filling and your energy expanding. You are standing inside a huge bubble full of the energy of unconditional love. You breathe it in, and it breathes you in. You become filled with love's energy. It is limitless, expansive, and free. Allow yourself to feel that protective bubble of love surround you, and feel your energy field expand.

Now imagine the energy of fear. Feel yourself step into that energy. Feel yourself surrounded and filled by fear. Notice how you respond.

The bubble of love is a few feet in front of you. Step into it again. Feel the love embrace you and soothe your fear. Know deep within your being that love is always that close.

Day 92

Second Attention

When we step out of everyday normal reality and into the realm of energy, we move into second attention. In second attention, we perceive things we wouldn't ordinarily see. Time has little meaning. Although we often drift in and out of second attention as we move through the day, we aren't always conscious of it.

Have you ever driven a familiar stretch of road and suddenly become aware, not knowing exactly where you are? Chances are you slipped into second attention. Learning how to consciously move into second attention makes feeling energy much easier. The Grandmother coached the young woman to go deeper, beyond her thoughts and emotions, to really listen to her body. Practice dropping down and feeling the energy around you. Notice the subtle changes that occur when you slip out of everyday awareness and into second attention.

DAY 93

Neutrality

What is neutrality? When you think of it, do you imagine an emotional void? Do you think of it as becoming numb?

Neutrality is really about attaining a sense of balance. When you achieve neutrality, you are fully alive and able to make choices based on love instead of fear. How would it feel to practice neutrality while talking about an emotionally charged issue?

The next time you find yourself in conversation about a topic that elicits strong emotions, practice neutrality. See how calmly you can discuss the issue. Neutrality doesn't mean you become numb; it is more a state of being that allows you to balance your emotions and choose how you want to act.

DAY 94

Power Moves

Feeling energy and using it to move your body is a very powerful way to transform yourself. Stand quietly with your legs shoulder width apart. Ask the energy to flow through you and to gently guide you. Raise your hands in front of you. Let your hands and body move, allowing the movements to be smooth and rhythmic. These power moves will feel almost like a graceful ballet.

Power moves are a form of moving meditation. They are very relaxing and energizing. If it feels appropriate you can play gentle music or light a candle. Just relax and let the energy move your body. Notice how it feels as it flows through you.

If you have a hard time feeling the guidance of the energy, start with your hands. Hold them in front of your face and move your right hand clockwise and your left hand counterclockwise. Move them very slowly and rhythmically in and out. Gently notice how that feels. Then sit in a chair and begin to move your legs in a circular motion, again noticing how it feels. Practice until you can feel the energy and let it move you. Relax into the energy, allowing it to move your body for about fifteen minutes. Then sit quietly for a few minutes.

DAY 95

Your Body

Take a few deep breaths and focus your attention on your body. Start at the top of your head and scan your entire length. Focus on each part of your body, noticing how it feels and whether it needs anything. Do you need to stretch? Do you need more rest? Does your body want different types of food or more water? Really listen to it.

How do you feel about your body? Do you treat your body in a sacred way? Do you take it for granted? Do you take time to nurture it? Do you love your body or judge it? What kind of relationship do you have with your body? Are there things about that relationship that you want to change? How might you start that process?

DAY 96

Death: A Meditation

Imagine standing on the shores of a faraway beach. The wind feels sharp and cold, and you pull your coat a little tighter. As you walk along reflecting about your life a dark figure approaches you. Your body shivers. It knows this visitor only too well.

As the figure stands beside you, he raises his hand and tells you that you need not fear; it is not your time to die. Death suggests you open your heart and your mind to his energy so you can experience it for what it is—a doorkeeper, a guide, and a teacher. You walk along with death and begin to feel it as a loving presence. You realize it always lives right at the edge of your consciousness. Allow yourself to be with the energy of death. Allow it to teach you.

DAY 97

Prayer

One of my favorite prayers is one attributed to St. Francis:

> God, make me the channel of Thy peace,
> Where there is hatred, let me bring Love,
> Where there is injury, pardon,
> Where there is doubt, faith,
> Where there is despair, hope,
> Where there is darkness, light,
> Where there is sadness, joy,
>
> May I not so much seek consolation as to console,
> to seek understanding as to understand,
> to seek love as to be loving.
>
> God, make me the channel of Thy peace,
> Where there is hatred, let me sow Love,
> For it is in giving, that we receive,
> and it is in pardoning, that we are pardoned,
> and it is in dying, that we are born to eternal life.

Some time ago a friend gave me a copy of this prayer and suggested I read it slowly and feel the energy behind it. Until then, my idea of prayer had been a one-way conversation in which I told the universe what I wanted, whether it was help or a quick fix.

Now I think of prayer as an opportunity for me to connect with my divinity and the divinity in everyone and everything.

Spend some time today in prayer. Allow yourself to feel the connection and then open your heart and your mind to the experience.

Day 98

Grief

When my mother died, I was grief stricken. I hadn't begun any inner exploration yet; at that point, to me, dead was dead. Grief is a process even when we know there is no such thing as loss. We often have an emotional response to the death of someone close to us.

I have watched people judge themselves for feeling sadness when a close friend died. Even though I can connect with pets or friends after they die, I still miss their physical presence. I allow myself to grieve as long as necessary. There is something delicious about emotions. They are neither good nor bad.

When I recapitulated my life, I was able to release the past once I grieved my losses. Grief is a process of letting go of the past. Until you allow yourself to grieve, you can never be free.

DAY 99

Time of Day

Pay attention to your energy level throughout the day. Get up before the sun and feel the energy of the dawn. Check in hourly and notice how your energy changes. What time of day do you feel most alert? When does your creativity peak? Watch the sun as it moves across the sky. What does midmorning feel like? When does the afternoon's energy start? How do you feel at dusk? How do you feel as you watch the sunset? What is your favorite part of the day?

DAY 100

Personal Power

Our energy is either contracting or expanding. When we are in touch with our personal power our energy expands. When we enter into personal importance, our energy contracts.

Moving into dominion with our world helps to connect us to our personal power. Whenever we judge others or ourselves, we are in personal importance. When we embrace life, we access our personal power. The Grandmother watched the women bathing and swimming in the waterfall and saw them filled with love and joy. The experience of personal importance and personal power are inversely proportionate.

How do you feel when you are in personal power? How does it affect your outlook and the choices you make?

As you move through the day notice whether you are in personal power or in personal importance. What causes you to move from one state to another?

DAY 101

Allies

When we confront some of our limiting beliefs, we often tend to seek out allies. A part of us may feel that if enough people agree with us, our beliefs must have merit.

Today seek out people who will likely disagree with your opinions. Notice whether you have any attachments to your point of view. Are you more comfortable with people who agree with you? If others disagree with you, do you find yourself wanting to convince them or questioning yourself?

Day 102

Petty Tyrants

Petty tyrants are those people, places, or things that we find disturbing but can't easily remove from our lives. They are our greatest teachers. I always tell my students that if they don't have a petty tyrant, they should go out and find one immediately. A petty tyrant has the ability to push our emotional buttons—perhaps that boss who can't be pleased or a friend who is always late. Petty tyrants assist us in seeing another piece of our filter system—if we are willing to look within.

Who or what is your most troubling petty tyrant? For today, view that person or thing as a welcome guest who has come to deliver a very important message to you. Then see if you can hear the message.

Day 103

Comfort Zone

People in the heating and air-conditioning industry often refer to the comfort zone: the amount the temperature can vary without people noticing or becoming uncomfortable. It's usually only a few degrees higher or lower.

In our lives we all have comfort zones. Things can vary up to a certain point and we won't mind, but go beyond that point and we react. Change always lies beyond our comfort zones. What can you do today that will take you out of your comfort zone? What can you do that will take you beyond the limitations of your mind?

day 104

Future Self: A Meditation

Your path wanders through fields covered with wildflowers. The clouds dance along occasionally caressing the mountaintops. In the distance a bird sings joyously. This path is well worn. Many have come before you and many will come after. You feel peaceful and at ease as you walk along.

In the distance a person begins to walk toward you. She seems strangely familiar. The figure is obviously older than you, and as she draws closer you realize she's your future self. She has come here to help you and thank you, for without the decisions you will make she wouldn't exist.

You embrace each other and walk along hand in hand. Your future self offers no advice but is more than willing to answer your questions. You talk for a long, long time. As your future self gets ready to leave, she turns and says, "If you remember nothing else, remember to always be gentle and loving with yourself. Your harsh inner voice serves you not."

Day 105

Observing

How do we observe without judging? How do we observe with clarity when we see through the distortion of our filter system? Imagine yourself standing in a place of clarity and neutrality, free of judgment. What would that feel like? Imagine yourself stepping beyond your filter system. How would the world look from there?

Observing the world around us and ourselves with clarity is a skill that takes practice. As soon as we have an emotional reaction or categorize something we have stopped observing. We have stepped behind the veil of our filter system. Practice visualizing yourself stepping beyond the confines of your filter system and truly observe.

day 106

Luminous Egg

When I look at someone's energy, I see a beautiful, luminescent egg with slender threads or filaments weaving over the surface. In some places there appear to be knots in the filaments. The egg extends about three feet beyond the person's body.

I first saw the egg one day when I was meditating. I recognized a good friend and a person with whom I was very angry standing side by side. Their energy looked exactly the same, and the image helped me reassess my anger.

It takes practice, but anyone can see that energy. We each "see" energy differently. Some people see images, some feel things, and others sense energy. Imagine seeing the energy of others. Be patient, practice, and eventually you will.

Day 107

Carry the Rock

You can simply carry a rock or you can carry the rock and all its weight. If you ask the rock whether it wishes to be moved and it agrees, you only have to carry it, not its weight. So it is with much of life. If you are in alignment with the intent of your highest spiritual essence, you will find yourself moving more easily through your days—your fears and burdens will not weigh you down.

Where in your life are you simply carrying the rock and where are you carrying the weight of the rock?

Day 108

Eating Mindfully

Food and mealtimes can provide more than just nourishment for your body. Let food nourish your whole being. Make a special meal for yourself, blessing the food as you prepare it. Sit down and eat slowly. As you chew each bite, think of all the people who made your meal possible. Thank the person who grew the seeds, the farmer, the banker, the trucker, the grocer, and yourself. Feel the sun, the earth, the rain, and the moon in every bite.

Eat mindfully.

DAY 109

Open to Receive

You can't fill a jar when the lid is screwed on. Imagine yourself open to receive all the love and abundance the universe so freely offers. How does it feel to be open to receive? How does it feel when your fear stops you from receiving?

Stop frequently today and notice whether you are open to receiving or closed. "Feel the spirit within you," the Grandmother said, "and surrender to the stillness you feel. Let go and let yourself drift in that endless sea of love."

Day 110

Mother Earth

The earth is our mother. She shelters us, nurtures us, and gives us life. Everything on this planet is part of the earth—the trees and the lakes of the countryside as well as the sidewalks and skyscrapers of our cities.

Take time today to give thanks to Mother Earth. As you walk on the grass or the pavement thank it for supporting you. Imagine a piece of your consciousness going to the center of the earth and feel your connection. Honor Mother Earth in your own way as you go about your day.

DAY III

Rocks

Because they are made of energy, as is everything on earth, even rocks have consciousness. Find a large rock and sit with it for a while. Imagine yourself becoming one with the rock.

When you go hiking, let the rocks guide your feet. As you become proficient at tuning in to the rocks, you will find you can maneuver them with greater ease and less fear of falling. Practice listening to rocks, and let them teach you to open yourself to the world around you and tune in with patience and understanding.

Day 112

Loving Yourself

Stand in front of a large mirror, look directly into your eyes, and connect with yourself. As you look into your eyes think of something that allows you to feel loving and then say to yourself, "I love you." Keep saying it to yourself until you really feel it and believe it.

We look into mirrors all the time, but how often do we really see ourselves and connect? Connect with yourself at least once a day and say something kind and loving to yourself.

chapter 5

And Then There Were Words

The Grandmother sat with her back against the tree noticing the signs of fall that surrounded her. The air had a slight chill and the sky shimmered a deep blue. Many of the birds had already flown south in preparation for winter. She felt the energy of the tree begin to stir. The Grandmother said a prayer of thanks, called upon the elements and the directions, and then opened herself up to the energy of the tree. Her body gently rocked as the energy of the tree flowed through her.

She found herself floating in that space between words. She could feel the energy of the acorns spread around the foot of the tree. Within each was the potential for a mighty oak, for the endless possibilities yet to come. The Grandmother became aware of a special kind of energy, full of ease and acceptance, expansive and immense. She felt no struggle, no fear; it was the energy of just being.

As she let herself become one with the tree, she relaxed totally and smiled. What peace. She let go and surrendered completely to the feeling.

When she opened her eyes it was already dark. She walked slowly back to the village where a group of children ran to her as she entered the square.

"We have much to talk about tonight, and it has nothing to do with words. Words can get in the way of the truth, they can cut us off from the source, but tonight I will use words to teach you how to go beyond them.

"At one time, we communicated with our hearts rather than our voices. We talked without words. The animals and the trees still remember how to do this, and they can teach you much.

"When we used our hearts instead of our minds, we used the language of love. When we depend on only words, we forget so much. We begin to see only with our eyes and forget to see with our hearts. Words can cause us to lose our connection with the very essence of life. We begin to see only physical reality and forget to look for the spirit or the love that is behind everything. We begin to believe in fear and forget that this is a safe universe; we stop seeing what is really real. We see the illusion of life instead of life itself.

"Words can cause us to lose that connection, but we can learn how to use words to remember and deepen it. The choice is ours. Use your words wisely. Use your words to open the door to the spirit and then stand in the silence and feel. Feel the energy behind everything, including your words. When you speak your words, what energy do you place in them? Are your words meant to hurt or to heal? Do you want your spirit to be seen, or do you use your words to hold up a mask? Only you can know the difference."

The Grandmother passed around some dried fruit and berries, the children's favorites. "I could give you these treats because I want you to love me or because I love you and want to share my bounty. The action would look the same to others, but the energy behind it would be very different. Could you tell? Could you really know what is in my heart?"

A little boy tentatively answered, "I think it would feel different."

"Yes, it would, my son. And if you wanted to be liked, you might agree to ignore the lie. I love myself so I don't need your love. I give my love freely because I give only of my overflow. Love yourselves and give always from a place of love. Love each other and listen to the whisperings of your heart. Go and be with nature. Let Mother Earth remind you that she only knows love and needs us not. Give yourself the greatest gift of all—remember the language of the heart."

DAY 113

Our Personal Myths

Each of us has a personal myth. It is the story we tell ourselves. Every morning we get up and remind ourselves all about our mythology. We remember who we are, how people treat us, whether the world is safe or hostile, whether we are loved and lovable. The list goes on and on.

What is your myth? Are you the hero or the victim? What role do you most often play in your life and in the lives of those about you?

Take some time and write the myth of your life. Then decide if you like the way the story is unfolding. Do you like the way it will end? If not, take some time to change your personal myth. Where would you like your life to go? You can choose to rewrite the myth of your life, starting now.

DAY 114

Wanting to Be Liked

Wanting to be liked is one of the biggest barriers to personal freedom. When we want to be liked, we make our decisions based on that desire rather than on what we wish to do. We give ourselves up in an attempt to gain the approval of others.

When we want others to like us, it is almost impossible to go inside and discover what we must do to take care of ourselves. Our sense of self matters little if our only quest is to be liked by others.

Today focus on liking yourself. Notice when your thoughts wander toward the opinions of others. Remind yourself that you matter more than anyone else. You are the most important person in your world.

DAY 115

Judgment

How do you feel when others judge you or you judge someone or something? Judgment, like domination, is often fear-based. In domination we need judgment so we can categorize everything. As long as our thinking is based in domination, we categorize things as good or bad, right or wrong, desirable or offensive.

In dominion we can allow things to simply be. Today, feel the energy of judgment as it operates in your life—at the office, at the grocery store, at home. Avoid judging your judgment. Just feel it for what it is. Notice how that energy feels to you. Simply observe.

When the Grandmother sat at the base of the oak tree, she was "aware of a special kind of energy, full of ease and acceptance, expansive and immense. She felt no struggle, no fear; it was the energy of just being."

Day 116

Guilt

When guilt is fear-based, we often use it to judge ourselves and feel like we have done something wrong. When it is love-based, we may regret our choices then move forward to look for another way we could have acted or other choices we could have made.

Guilt can cause us to feel bad about ourselves or assist us in seeing the roles we played in a situation. Once we see our roles with clarity and without blame, we may find it easier to make different choices in the future.

What role does guilt play in your life? Are you willing to use it as a tool of love in the future?

DAY 117

Ideal World: A Meditation

As you begin to wake up you realize you live in the ideal world; in it, everything is perfect. You are the ruler of your world, and you decide what to do and when to do it. You never *have* to do anything and there isn't anything you *should* do. When you need to decide your next activity, you go inside, connect with your inner wisdom, and ask yourself for guidance. In this ideal world there are no tasks waiting to be accomplished. You feel so free and so grateful to be living in this ideal world.

For a moment you think about the world you used to live in, a world full of guilt and anger. There you were driven by things you had to or should do. Your self-worth depended on other people's opinions and what you accomplished in life. You drift back to sleep.

As you wake up from your dreams you realize you have a choice. Today you can live in heaven or hell. You can decide what you want to do or what you have to do. The choice is yours and it all depends on which world you choose to live in.

day 118

Dogma

A man asked his wife why she always cut off the end of the roast before she put it in the pan. She replied, "Because that is how my mother taught me." So he asked his mother-in-law why she cut off the end of her roast, and she replied, "Because that is how my mother taught me." When the man asked his wife's grandmother why she did so, she replied, "Because that was the only way it would fit in my pan."

Dogma in any form is limiting. Just because a particular technique worked in the past, it may not be the best solution for the present. Notice whether you have any dogma lurking in your life.

DAY 119

Mitote

The *mitote* refers to the chaos and noises of the marketplace. Our untrained minds are very much like a visit to a busy marketplace. Our thoughts run wild, each one clamoring for our attention. Quieting the *mitote* of the mind is one of the objectives of the Toltec path.

Think of your mind as a train station. See yourself standing on the platform watching your thoughts go by. Occasionally you take a ride on one of your thoughts, but as soon as you notice, you can get off again, and watch your thoughts go by. You may get on and off hundreds of times a day. As long as you keep getting off, you will eventually train your mind to wait for you to tell it what to do.

Today think of your thoughts as trains and watch them go by. Hop on the ones that intrigue you, but remain aware that you can disembark a particular thought at any moment.

DAY 120

Gossip

Gossip is one of the most powerful ways to spread emotional poison. Whenever we talk about someone else, positively or negatively, we are gossiping.

Often we share our beliefs about someone in an attempt to create allies. We want people to agree with us, to see the world as we do, so we can reaffirm our filter system. Gossip has an energy component behind it that is unmistakable. When my energy is open and expansive, vulnerable and focused on deepening my connection with another, I am not likely to gossip. But when I strive to look good or get another to like me, my energy is contracting. If I have an emotional wall up, there is a good chance the energy of gossip is present in my communications.

Notice what the energy of gossip feels like. The Grandmother asked "When you speak your words, what energy do you place in them? Are your words meant to hurt or to heal?" Notice how often gossip is present in your life.

DAY 121

Fear

What is your biggest fear? Being homeless, having people make fun of you, dying, being overcome by a crippling illness? Bring up your fear, really allow yourself to feel it fully in your body.

How does your body feel? How is your breathing? Take a moment to notice the energy state of your body.

Mentally play out the scenario of your greatest fear. What is the worst possible thing that could happen? Is that what you really want to create? Probably not. What would you *like* to create instead?

DAY 122

The Garden: A Meditation

The walls are covered with ivy and the weathered gate is barely visible through the overgrowth. Its handle is worn smooth by the many hands that have pushed it open. The air smells moist and carries the scent of herbs and flowers, adding to the garden's quiet, sacred quality.

As the gate closes behind you, your eyes adjust to the shifting light. You find yourself in a small courtyard filled with ferns. A moss-covered fountain splashes in the courtyard's center. You sit down on the bench, take your shoes off, and run your toes through the grass. Your eyes pause at the statue of the goddess among the flowers, and you give thanks for this beautiful sanctuary.

You know this is a place of great wisdom where you could talk to the goddess and ask about anything. Sit and allow the love to wash over you, giving thanks.

DAY 123

Emotional Poison

We can poison our environment with our anger and fear. Our emotional wounds act like bodily infections. The emotional poison can seep into our lives.

Gossip is one of the many ways we spread that poison. If someone pokes at one of your emotional wounds, you may feel angry and betrayed; in response, you tell anyone who will listen how terrible that person is. You've just spread your infection.

Will you use your emotions as weapons to hurt yourself and others, or as guideposts to freedom? Today if you find yourself starting down the path of spreading poison through gossip, stop and change your direction. Infect your life with positive energy instead of emotional poison.

DAY 124

Inner Dialogue

We are constantly talking to ourselves. Our inner dialogue can be loving or judgmental. Today listen to how you talk to yourself, what you tell yourself, and how many opinions you have about your world.

Set your intent to make your inner dialogue as loving, expansive, and supportive as possible.

DAY 125

Discouragement

We are often willing to let go of old and familiar ways of doing things only after we become completely discouraged. Only after we fully recognize that the old ways don't work do we become willing to try something different.

We often think of discouragement as something to avoid, but it's not. The sooner we get discouraged with our old behaviors, the sooner we will become willing to let them go. Make discouragement your friend. Welcome it into your life as a messenger or precursor of change. Invite it into your life so you can let go of your limitations.

DAY 126

Them and Us

Domination fosters the concept of duality: you and I, them and us. How often do you feel like it's you against the world? How often do you think in terms of them and us? How would your world be different if you experienced yourself as part of the great mystery instead of as a separate entity? When the Grandmother "let herself become one with the tree, she relaxed totally and smiled. What peace. She let go and surrendered completely to the feeling." Notice how often you feel a sense of separation today.

DAY 127

Leaking Energy

We each have our favorite ways to leak energy. Some of us worry, some get angry or overly busy. Leaking energy is often a way to avoid an issue or an action that might be uncomfortable. Perhaps we decide to meditate every morning but instead find ourselves spending an hour on the computer.

Observe how you leak energy and what triggers your desire to do so. Just observing where your energy leaks are can set you on the way to plugging them.

Day 128

Growing: A Meditation

You are a tiny seed nestled in the warm soil of spring. The rains come, and as you begin to swell, a tiny sprout of life begins to push from the center of your being. Your roots dive down into the soil, securing you in the earth, providing you with nourishment and water. Your stem reaches up to the fresh, warm air. Your leaves gently unfurl and follow the path of the sun through the sky. Feel the new life flowing through you. Feel the growth of spring enrich you.

DAY 129

Betrayal

Everything in life is a gift—it is up to us to unwrap each gift and use it in our lives.

We all know what betrayal feels like, but what is it really? The emotions that betrayal evokes are so primal they seem to go to our very core. Once we learn to view betrayal differently, those emotions can become a gateway toward greater intimacy and a deeper connection to ourselves.

When I look at betrayal, I can focus my attention on what I perceive as treachery or I can look at my own expectations. Whenever I have an expectation, I set myself up to be disappointed, especially if my expectations are not clear to me or to the people around me. I must clearly negotiate and define my expectations. Are they realistic?

Many of us have had the unrealistic expectation that people will treat us differently than they treat others. They might lie to everyone else, but we expect they will tell us the truth. They will cheat on their former lovers, but we expect they will be faithful to us. They will gossip about other people, but we expect they will keep our secrets. When they don't treat us differently and meet our expectations, we feel betrayed. But people are consistent unless they are actively working on changing a behavior.

I have found that if I base my happiness on another person, I eventually feel let down or betrayed. Ultimately I am the only person responsible for my happiness. If I expect my friends, lovers, or the world as a whole to make me happy, I doom myself to a life filled with disappointments. On the other hand, if I realize I am in charge of my happiness, I can be happy regardless of the events in my life. Focusing on the feeling of betrayal prevents me from looking at what role my beliefs and expectations play in the creation of my happiness.

If I turn my attention from what happened to what I can change—myself and my reactions—life can become one magical experience after another. Even the most profound betrayal can be my greatest guide, an opportunity for me to deepen my connection with myself. I can understand my expectations, see how they affect my choices, and choose anew. As I look within, I learn to listen to my inner voice, to trust myself, and to clearly understand my expectations.

DAY 130

Words

Words tend to limit our experience of the energy. Once we start talking to ourselves and listening to what we say, we are no longer in the moment. We no longer experience the energy called life and begin to live in our minds instead. Words take us out of the moment. "Words can cause us to lose our connection with the very essence of life," the Grandmother said. The more belief we have attached to a word or label, the more limiting it is.

Some words are more emotionally loaded than others. Notice how you feel when you think of words like *love, betrayal, right, wrong, should, have to.* . . . Carry a notepad and jot down your favorite words while you notice your associations with them. Change what you have attached to certain loaded words and see what happens.

DAY 131

What's Working

Do you have a tendency to focus on what isn't working in your life or what you would like to change? Today notice what you love about your life and what *is* working. Track those things. Observe those actions that are effective and do more of them. Then take it a step further and use those skills in other areas of your life.

DAY 132

Change

Change is one of the few constants in life. How do you feel about change? Is it something you embrace, or do you resist it? Does change frighten you? What are your beliefs about change?

How have you approached change in the past? What would you like to alter about the process of change?

Think of a time you made a change in your life that was easy. What did you do? Now think of a time you were unable to change something. What did you do then?

DAY 133

Being

What does the concept of being mean to you? What does it feel like? What is a being? What does being a human being mean? Explore the concept of being for yourself.

Take a moment to just be who you are alone. Notice your surroundings and just be there. And when you are with others today, take the time to really be with them. Listen to them, take a deep breath, and look deeply into their eyes. Practice being wholly with them. Pets are wonderful creatures to practice being with—they do it so naturally.

DAY 134

Savoring Life: A Meditation

You have only a couple of bites left of your favorite dessert. You take one piece and derive full pleasure in the taste. Chewing it slowly, you relish every little bit of it. You take another, aware that you have only one bite left. Take your time and hold it in your mouth as long as you can. It is so delicious. Finally, take the last bite, close your eyes, and allow yourself to fully savor it.

Now imagine yourself slowly waking up in the morning. Enjoy the feeling of awakening. You get up and move about your day enjoying the gift of every moment. Savor your life, squeezing every bit of joy out of each moment.

Take time to savor life's little joys as well as the pain. When you eat mindfully, you can enjoy each mouthful. When you shower, feel the water run sensuously over your body. You take time to notice the clouds, the sun, the rain, and the stars. Go out and embrace the light of the moon. You give thanks for the gift of your senses, and you use them fully.

Take time to live each moment and savor all of life in the process.

Day 135

Listening

When someone speaks to you today just listen. Normally we busy ourselves thinking about what the person is saying and formulating our reply. We seldom just listen.

Listen to the sounds around you. When people speak to you, pretend you don't understand the language. Try not to get caught up in the words; listen to the sounds and feel the energy behind them. Disengage your mind and listen with your heart.

Practice listening rather than thinking.

DAY 136

Letters

Unsent letters offer a wonderful way to dispose of emotional garbage. Write a letter to God, your lover, your best friend, your parents, the first person who broke your heart, or anyone else you have emotional ties to.

Today write at least one letter and then let the emotions go. Let the letter be as messy and your words as judgmental as you like; let all the emotions flow out of you and onto the page with the intent of letting go. Then use the letter in a ceremony of healing. Burn it or tear it into little pieces.

DAY 137

Being Powerful

My definition of power and my relationship to it has changed immensely over the years. At first the thought of being powerful terrified me. But once I realized I could be powerful, loving, and gentle simultaneously, my fear left me.

How do you feel about being a powerful person? What does that mean to you? How do you define power? What is your relationship to power?

Day 138

Trust

Trust is a funny thing. It isn't necessarily an external thing. Learning to trust yourself and your inner knowledge is one of the most important things you can do for yourself.

When people work with me, I warn them not to trust me. That may seem a contradiction to my belief that the universe is safe, but it's not. Let me explain. If you trust me, you may ignore your own inner guidance. If you believe people will disappoint you, you'll only trust them when they are likely to disappoint you. You'll expect me to do something, and not hear me when I tell you what I'm actually going to do. Then you'll be disappointed.

Once you learn to trust yourself, you'll be more trustworthy as well. You won't set people up to disappoint you.

If you ask someone who has failed you in the past to do something and he agrees, listen to the little voice that warns, "He will forget." Ignoring that voice is a wonderful way to get to be right, disappointed, and angry. If you don't listen to and trust your inner knowing, then trusting someone else will set you up for disappointment.

Learn to listen to your inner voice. Once you do you'll realize you can always trust people to be consistent.

Day 139

Eulogy

Write your own eulogy. What do you want people to say about you after your death? Read your eulogy to someone you care deeply about.

Write about the experience.

DAY 140

A Letter to Yourself

If you could talk to the person you were five years ago, what would you say? What do you know now that could have helped you then?

Imagine yourself ten years from now. What might that person know that could help you now? Imagine that future you writing you a letter. Now sit down, write it, and mail it to yourself. When it arrives read it with an open mind and heart.

chapter 6

Awakening

The Grandmother's spirit raced faster than time, to the very edge of the universe, to the home of the ancestors. She stood at the edge of a magnificent cliff watching and waiting. All around her the elements raged. The wind howled, the waves churned, crashing onto the cliff below her, lightning chased the darkness, and the earth trembled. Yet she felt no fear.

She raised her arms above her head and shouted, "I am here."

For a moment the wind became still and she listened. Lightning continued to strike all around her. She smiled as the wind howled once more. There was no other response.

So again she held her hands aloft and shouted, "I am here. Great Spirit, hear my words. I have come to be with you. I have traveled far and my journey brings me to you."

The earth shook; the Grandmother felt herself falling, and she rejoiced. Her spirit began to fly with a freedom and joy unlike any she had known before.

She flew until she came to a beautiful valley with a stream running through it, nestled between two magnificent mountains. She sat down and watched the sunlight filter through the canopy of trees. A leaf drifted down the stream, dancing around rocks and over small waterfalls. She heard a bird sing and watched a butterfly float by. The air smelled sweetly of the fragrance of honeysuckle.

A bear walked slowly toward her, yet she felt no fear. The bear stood directly before the Grandmother and raised his massive paw. His claws were fully extended when he reached out and touched her face. With a rich and melodic voice he said, "It is good you know no fear, my child. Fear stops us from feeling the love that lives in everything. The physical world as you know it is all energy and that energy is love. Fear not and you will be able to feel the love; walk in fear and you will not know the love. Awaken to your true nature. You are a perfect spirit made of pure, unconditional love. Awaken to who and what you really are, and fear will never again be able to grip your heart and your mind.

"Stand up and look at your body. What do you see? Allow yourself to see what is, rather than what you expect to see."

The Grandmother looked down and saw a beautiful luminescent egg. It shimmered. The surface danced with iridescent colors that sparkled and swirled with each breath she took. She was pure light; she was love and laughter.

The bear pointed at the water, and as the Grandmother looked at the surface she saw her village. Instead of people, she saw beings of light. Even those who treated the rest of the village with contempt shimmered as they walked. She saw strands of light emanating from every person. The village looked like a huge light show, a spider web that glowed as it moved and changed and grew.

The Grandmother saw how all actions affect the whole. She saw how anger restricted the energy and love seemed to untangle even the biggest knots. No matter what each person did or said, the energy reflected the truth. She saw how people could follow the energy lines, how they could use them as guideposts to make even the hardest of times easy. The Grandmother watched and learned much.

Slowly, the Grandmother became aware of herself, sitting at the edge of the ceremonial circle. All eyes were upon her. It was her time to speak. She looked at the energy of those gathered around her and realized she had much to say.

DAY 141

Having a Sense of Humor

Having a sense of humor makes the process of attaining personal freedom much easier. We often take ourselves entirely too seriously. You can have compassion for the emotional turmoil you're going through and still be able to laugh. You can see the humor without making fun of yourself.

Imagine yourself as an actor in a movie. What if you saw your life as a comedy instead of a drama? Rent some comedies. Laugh. Lighten up and engage your sense of humor. Try to laugh instead of getting angry or afraid today. Let yourself see the humor in life.

DAY 142

Definitions

Write your definitions for the following:

Love ....

Fear ....

Vulnerability ....

Joy ....

Freedom ....

Happiness ....

Work ....

Play ....

Control ....

Emotions ....

Actions ....

Responsibility ....

Fault ....

Right ....

Wrong ....

Good ....

Evil ....

God ....

How do these definitions affect your responses to the events in your life?
    How dedicated are you to defending your definitions? Are you willing to change them if they limit your experience?

Day 143

Assumptions

Our minds are cluttered with assumptions. Observe just how many assumptions you make. What do you assume you know? How do you assume others should act? How many rules do you have about life? Notice the multiple roles assumptions play in your life.

Challenge your assumptions. Practice not making assumptions and see what difference it makes in how you approach your life.

DAY 144

Resistance

Gravity allows us to push against the earth so we can move forward. Without the resistance of gravity, it would be very difficult to move around. As we explore our filter system, we often run into resistance. You can view resistance as a negative experience, use it as an excuse to go no farther, or use it to assist you in moving along your path.

How much resistance do you experience to change? What do you do with that resistance? How could you use it as a tool? Do you resist the idea of embracing your resistance?

Day 145

Fault

"What is wrong with me? How could I have been so stupid, or petty, or judgmental?" Those are the kinds of questions we ask ourselves when fault is present in our thinking. Blame and fault lead us back into domination. They don't lead us toward our divinity.

Notice today how often you feel fault rising to the surface of your consciousness. When you do, embrace it, thank it for coming, and then explore how you can transform it. How can you respond differently to the event?

day 146

The Judge

Each of us has a voice I call the judge. It judges everything and everyone. The judge has only one job: to judge. It isn't our job to judge the judge. If we embrace that voice, we can detach and decide moment by moment whether we want to listen to it.

In this moment do you want to listen to the judge or would you rather change stations and listen to the voice of love instead? If you judge your judgments, you are no closer to achieving freedom.

Do you want to continue listening to the voice of the judge?

Day 147

Waking Up: A Meditation

Your consciousness drifts lazily, half asleep. You roll over and go back to sleep. You dream that your choices are limited. You know fear, people you care about die, and some even betray you. You are surrounded by beauty, sounds, and intoxicating smells. The dream seems real and absorbs you into the action. So many stories, so many emotions, and so many choices you fail to see. You no longer want to wake up. The dream pulls you further and further into its illusion, and you become very attached to it.

You know you are a spirit and that you're in a dream, yet it is hard to awaken. You struggle and fight with yourself until one day you finally surrender. You embrace everything about the dream, and in that instant you wake up.

You stretch, get up out of bed, and reach for your dream journal. What a wonderful dream. To get so completely attached to an illusion that you could forget your limitless nature. What fun dreaming is—you can experience what you aren't and awaken with deeper gratitude for what you really are.

day 148

Motives

One of the paradoxes I've observed is that if I do my inner explorations in order to get something, it doesn't seem to work very well. If I attempt to connect with my divinity in order to get a better job or have a more loving relationship, it never seems to work. On the other hand, if I clear out my filter system and use these tools in order to connect with my true essence, suddenly I find myself with a magical life, a wonderful job, and loving relationships. I've learned to monitor my motives.

What are your motives for walking this path?

DAY 149

Choices

How do you make your choices? Are you aware of how profoundly your filter system affects your choices?

What choices are you going to make about today? How do you want to feel when you go to bed tonight? What choices do you need to make moment by moment if you want to feel that way tonight? Observe your choices today; notice how you made them and how mindful you were as you made them.

DAY 150

Power

When I first started thinking about power, I thought of things like control and manipulation. My definition of power was contaminated with domination. As I infused my definition of power with dominion, it became something desirable, loving, and supportive.

How do you define power? Are you comfortable with becoming a powerful person? Does being powerful carry undue responsibilities or does being powerful actually increase your ability to respond? Does having power seem freeing or constricting?

If the idea of being powerful makes you fearful, realize that your definition is based in domination and change your definition. Work with your ideas about power until it becomes light and freeing.

DaY 151

Freedom

What does freedom feel like? "The earth shook; the Grandmother felt herself falling, and she rejoiced. Her spirit began to fly with a freedom and joy unlike any she had known before."

We are limitless beings, totally free, yet how often is that our experience?

Play with the concept of freedom today. What would freedom feel like in your life? Approach the idea of freedom with curiosity. We know what limitations feel like—today experiment with freedom. How do you stop yourself from experiencing freedom? Notice how often your mind limits your experience.

DAY 152

Communication

We think we use words to communicate, yet most of our communications are nonverbal. "What do you want?" is a simple series of words, but depending on the energy we put behind them those words can mean many things. Those four words can express anything from love and support to disdain and rejection.

Begin to notice the energy component of your verbal communications. Try saying *you* but change the meaning by changing the energy you put behind it. Say the word *you* as many different ways as you can. *You* can be a term of endearment, judgment, or indifference. Experiment saying words with love, anger, fear, or sadness. Ask a friend to listen to you as you look at them and simply say *you*. Try to get them to "feel" the different emotions as you say the word. Play with the energy you place behind the words.

Day 153

Horse Ride: A Meditation

In front of you stands the most magnificent horse. Her eyes are full of love and understanding, and you feel completely relaxed in her presence. You stand nose to nose breathing each other's essence. When she nuzzles against your body, you throw your arms around her neck.

Suddenly you find yourself on her back, riding. The countryside rushes by as she leaps upward, and you begin to fly. You feel safe flying far above the rooftops. You look down and see the clouds below you. The horse's muscles ripple beneath you. You can feel her strength and courage surge through you.

You come to rest in the middle of a beautiful meadow. You dance and laugh until you can't dance anymore; then you gently drop to the ground. The smell of wildflowers fills your heart as you watch the clouds drift freely by. You slip into the beauty and the freedom of the moment. You are free and you realize you always have been. The walls of your prison have been your thoughts; you let them drift by like the clouds, knowing they can't hold you any longer.

DAY 154

Celebration

Celebrate your discoveries as you become more aware of who and what you are. You are who you are. You have a light side and a shadow self. Neither is better, they are just different aspects of the totality of you. Without the total you, the universe would be incomplete.

Think of the energy of celebration. The next time you become aware of a limiting part of your filter system, celebrate the awareness as well as the filter. If you find yourself despairing over not spending more time with an elderly parent, celebrate your awareness but don't judge yourself. Judgment in no way facilitates change. Judgment actually acts like cosmic superglue. Learn to celebrate all of life—your lighter self, your darker self, your filter system, and the things that kick your filter system into gear—and see what happens.

DAY 155

Praise

Raise your right hand over your head. Turn your hand so it faces behind you. Now reach down and pat yourself on the back. Praise yourself regularly throughout the day. Honor yourself as the magnificent being of light that you really are. Let the love in. Do this at least once every day.

DAY 156

Speaking Your Truth

What is your truth? How do you feel about telling people what you really believe in? What is your truth today versus ten years ago? How do you think your truth will change in the next six months? Is your truth "the truth"? Is it static, or do you allow it to change and grow with you?

During the course of the day, ask yourself what your truth is about any given situation, and then ask yourself what other truth you could tell yourself.

DAY 157

Floating Down the River: A Meditation

It is a warm summer day. The sunlight filtering through the tree branches speckles the surface of the water as you lazily float down the river on a huge inner tube. The river flows slowly between its broad banks. You dangle your hand in the water and watch the water drops fall from your fingers. Totally at peace and at ease, you lay back and enjoy the ride. The sounds of the birds and the lapping of the water lull you to sleep.

The noise of the rapids ahead causes you to stir. You set your intent to go around a rock, lean on one side of the inner tube, and notice how it gently steers in that direction. As if doing a graceful dance, you weave your way through the rapids. You enjoy the excitement and when you've passed the rapids, you settle back on your inner tube. You think about how floating down the river is so much easier than swimming against the current.

Day 158

Mindfulness

Mindfulness refers to a state of being in which we become fully present in the moment. Take a deep breath and allow yourself to be mindful of this moment. Notice your surroundings, the sensations in your body; let go of your thoughts and just be right here right now.

Become mindful of your breathing. Focus your full attention on your breath. Follow the air as it moves in and out of your lungs, feel your chest as it rises and falls, and notice the lift of your stomach. Take three deep breaths. Now how do you feel? Bring mindfulness to as many of your activities as you can today.

DAY 159

Generosity

Are you generous of spirit or miserly? Do you give freely of your time and your love or do you hoard them? One of my spiritual mentors told me to give freely to others but only of my overflow. Make sure your cup is always full and then give of yourself.

Do something every day that fills your heart and soul. Fill yourself up and then be generous of spirit with others. But begin with being generous to yourself. Do you freely give yourself the time you need to recharge? Do you give love freely to yourself?

Today, practice being generous of spirit with yourself.

day 160

The Shadows in the Sounds

As a species we tend to focus on the light rather than on the shadows. But the shadows give things depth. For months I had been working with shadows. I found them fascinating. I had spent countless hours trying to hear the shadows in the sounds, the silence that surrounds the sounds.

One cold, clear, predawn morning I took my dog for a walk. The sky was just turning pink over the mountains and the ocean glistened in the starlight. Then a bird in a yucca tree sang its first notes to greet the coming day. I stood transfixed as I heard the shadows in its song, and sounds were never the same again. Being able to hear the shadows gave even the most mundane sound another dimension.

Start listening for the shadows. Close your eyes, take a deep breath, and listen for the spaces between the sounds. Once you can hear them, listen for the shadows in your thoughts.

DaY 161

Personal Tape Recorder

Carry around a small tape recorder, and every time you have a judgmental thought record it. Judgmental thoughts can be as simple as "It's hot" or "It's cold" or "Look at that woman's outfit." Judgments come in all shapes and sizes. We can even judge ourselves for being judgmental. Be aware of how quickly the tape fills up. Every time you use the tape recorder, remember to replace your judgmental thought with a loving one. If you start to judge yourself, instead, be grateful for noticing your judgments.

When you have filled the tape, do a ceremony to release all of your judgments. Ask the universe to help you be more loving and less fearful until judgment is a thing of the past.

DAY 162

I Know

Think of the phrase *I know*—it may seem harmless but as soon as we say it, we close the door to any other answers because we already know. That simple phrase locks you into in your assumptions, your beliefs, and your agreements. *I know* solidifies your filter system. You can't fill a cup that is already full.

Notice how often you say "I know" to yourself or others. Even if you don't speak the words how often do you feel the comfort of knowing the answers? Observe the depth of what you believe you know.

Today practice saying "I don't know." Say it often and loud and clearly. Say "I don't know" especially when you really think you know the answer. See how you feel when you say "I don't know." Just for today have an empty cup and see how life fills it.

Day 163

Circle of Friends: A Meditation

Deep within the forest is a clearing used only for special ceremonies. You stand at the edge of the clearing under a full moon, soaking in the magic and wonder of the place. Fireflies flit around and the wind rustles the leaves.

You sense that you are not alone and as you step out of the shadows into the circle you realize others are joining you. The person to your right lovingly takes your hand and you offer your other hand to the person on your left. In a moment you are all holding hands in a circle of light.

You feel the love and the power as it circulates around and around. As a group, you step forward and hold your hands aloft. You humbly offer your heart to the love of the universe and realize you will always stand in a circle of friends.

day 164

Sacred Self

When we connect with our sacred self all of life suddenly changes. Where we saw cruelty we now see opportunity. That which angered us becomes a gateway to freedom. Everything is the same and yet nothing has the same meaning. "The Grandmother's spirit raced faster than time, to the very edge of the universe, to the home of the ancestors."

Connecting with your sacred self is a process. Be loving and gentle as you explore your feelings of separation. Create a daily routine of things that help you connect with the sacred part of you, be generous of spirit with yourself and others, and allow every event in your life to bring you closer to your sacred self.

You are either moving toward your divinity or reaffirming your fears. As you move through your day ask yourself, "Is this the voice of love or fear?" If it is the voice of fear, be gentle and loving with yourself and choose again. It takes practice to connect with your divinity.

day 165

I'm Honored to Be in Your Presence

Every morning look into the mirror and tell yourself that you are honored to be in your presence.

This exercise is very powerful when done in a group. Form a circle. Have each person in turn walk around the circle, look deeply into each participant's eyes, take a moment to really connect, and then say, "I am honored to be in your presence." Notice whether it is harder for you to say or to hear.

Day 166

Quiet, Still Voice

Your mind, your small self, your personal importance is raucous and will try to convince you with a sales pitch. Your true self never will. Your spirit, your inner wisdom, the essence of who and what you are always speaks to you as a quiet, still voice. It will make gentle suggestions.

Today notice that quiet, still voice and really listen to it.

Day 167

True Nature

There are no absolutes. There is no such thing as the truth. The truth changes as your perspective changes. Your true nature keeps changing as well. In my twenties I would have described my true nature as a fun-loving, free-spirited, party girl. After my mom died I wasn't sure who I was or what my life was about. Today I allow the concept of my true nature to be fluid. I know that my true nature is beyond my understanding. It is loving and compassionate and expansive in ways I can only begin to imagine. To the best of my ability, on a daily basis I align myself with that true nature.

Today, allow yourself to connect with your true nature and be guided by that connection. Think about how your true nature has changed in your life and embrace the fact that it will change again.

Day 168

Connecting with Your Spirit

Take a deep breath and settle down into your body. Focus on breathing in through the bottoms of your feet. Imagine your breath being drawn up from the center of the earth. As you breathe, allow your consciousness to go deeper and deeper into your body. Literally feel your consciousness sinking down into your body. Breathe yourself into the very center of your being. Practice this often as you go about the day.

We live so much of our lives in our heads. Getting out of your consciousness, out of your head, and into your heart are important steps in the process of connecting with your spirit. I used to struggle with this because I was so thought oriented. Now it is as simple as taking a breath. Close your eyes, relax, let go, and breathe. Get out of your head and into your heart.

chapter 7

Beyond the Mists

She became aware of herself for the first time. She looked at the mists swirling around her and knew she was everywhere and nowhere. She was everyone and no one.

"Who am I?"

A rich, melodic voice full of love answered, "You are my creation and I am well pleased."

"Who are you?" asked the woman.

"I am that which existed before time and will exist long after. I am all there is. I am that which gives life and meaning to everything. I am love."

The woman could feel the meaning of those words fill her and she knew love.

"Why am I here?"

"You are an explorer. You are here to remember. You will explore the universe, remembering who and what you are as well as what you aren't. In order to fully remember yourself as love, you will have to find out what love is not. Then you will be free to choose—love or fear."

The mists thinned and in the distance the woman could see beauty beyond her wildest imaginings. She moved toward the beauty and the mists began to part.

"As long as you are on this side of the mists you can see both worlds. As soon as you step out of the mist and into the physical world, you will forget who and what you are. You will forget even me. You will leave your home and then it is up to you. But remember, my child, you can always come home again."

A tear formed in the woman's eye. "But how will I remember? How will I find my way home?"

"You are a limitless being of light, but the limitations of fear, anger, sadness, and anything else that constricts the flow of your energy will push you to remember. You will rebel against those limitations and eventually you will find their causes. Eventually you will realize that your beliefs caused your experience of separation. You may forget for a long time, but bit by bit you will remember that physical reality is an illusion. One day you will realize that reality lies beyond what your eyes see, that reality lives in the land of the mists. Then you will be free to live in both worlds simultaneously."

The woman moved forward and the mist began to clear. She looked down and felt the warmth of the sun on her body. She took a deep breath and smelled the air heavy with the scent of the morning dew and the flowers covering the hillside.

"Fear contracts while love expands. You are love so your spirit will chafe against the limits fear puts on it. Fear will always lead you back to love.

"I will always be with you. I will be a quiet, still voice whispering to you, reminding you that you are loved, reminding you that I am love."

The woman was no longer listening. Her attention was fully hooked by her five senses. She ran feeling the soft ground under her feet. She squealed in delight. She fell down on the ground and smelled the earth and the flowers. She rolled over and looked up at the sky mesmerized by the clouds.

The woman walked all day; she saw many animals and enjoyed all the beauty. As the sun set she sat on the edge of a cliff and looked around. In that moment she knew she had forgotten something; she realized she was alone, and she knew fear.

The wind stirred and she thought she heard a voice saying, "You are never alone. I am always with you in your heart. I am love."

The woman began to chant a prayer to the evening sun asking it to return again in the morning. She smiled as she drifted off to sleep, taking comfort in the quiet, still voice she heard in her heart.

day 169

Allowing for the Possibility

Anything is possible if we are willing to let it be.

Allow for the possibility that you can perceive and experience the events in your life differently. As you move through your day ask yourself:

- How can I see this differently?
- If I am distressed, how can I see this event so I feel at peace?
- If I am at peace, how can I see this event so I feel distressed?

We are attached to seeing the world a certain way, but if our life doesn't conform to that picture, we become unhappy.

Allowing for the possibility is a very powerful exercise. Instead of reacting to events in your life allow for the possibility that:

- you can act differently regardless of what is happening.
- there really is no "out there."
- nothing is real.
- everything is real.

Then notice what you want to hold onto and what you want to let go of. Let yourself remember that we are often most attached to the very things that limit us. As Buddha said, it is our attachment that is the root of our suffering.

Spend the day allowing for the possibility that everyone else in the world is enlightened except you and see what happens. It can be very enlightening!

DAY 170

Choosing Love or Fear

We can always choose, even though sometimes it doesn't feel that way. It takes time, practice, and a few skinned knees to learn how to ride a bicycle. But once we learn, we never forget.

So it is with our emotions. We can learn to change how we feel, but it will take some practice. Take a few deep breaths. Really focus on feeling your breath and allow it to take you within.

Think about something that allows you to feel all warm and fuzzy inside—a baby, a puppy, a kitten, a sunset, your beloved—whatever helps you to generate that feeling of love within you.

Now think of something that allows you to feel fear. Let that fear well up inside of you. Then go back to love. Practice shifting between the two emotions until it becomes easy and effortless for you. The next time you find yourself angry or upset about something, shift gears and step into love. See if it makes a difference in your perception of the event.

DAY 171

Your Birth: A Meditation

You float in the warmth of the womb completely at peace, completely at ease. You sleep and dream about your new life. Suddenly the warm water is gone and violent contractions force you down a narrow opening. You feel fear for the first time. You're squeezed tighter and tighter until you are thrust into the world. It is so bright, and your lungs hurt as you take your first breath.

At first you scream loudly, but then you feel a presence around you. There are beings of light surrounding you. They reach out in love and touch your head and your heart.

They whisper in your ear, "We are always here right at the edge of your consciousness. All you have to do is ask for our help and we will always be there for you. Remember. Remember your divinity. Remember to feel the love all around you."

They lay you on your mother's breast. You hear her familiar heartbeat and feel safe again. Look at the light beings around you and know you are loved.

Day 172

Boundaries

I once saw a letter to God from a little boy who wanted to know who put the boundaries around countries. We can use boundaries to limit our experience or to give us a greater sense of freedom to navigate our world.

We often use boundaries unconsciously to reinforce our filter system. For example, if we fear intimacy, we may unconsciously use boundaries to keep people from getting too close. What do boundaries mean to you? How do you use them, consciously and unconsciously? How can you use them to create a deeper connection to your divinity?

Early morning is my time to connect with my spirituality and myself, and I use boundaries to keep that time sacred. For instance, instead of answering the phone in the morning, I'll let voicemail pick up. Or if someone asks me to do something in the morning, I lovingly explain it's my special time of day—a time I leave for myself.

Day 173

Power Places

There are places on this planet that speak to our spirits in ways nothing else can. The ocean speaks to some while the desert calls others. Listen to your spirit. Find your own power places. "You are an explorer. You are here to remember."

When I lived in San Diego, I often went to the beach, but I also found a place in the desert that really fed my soul. Whenever I travel I let my spirit guide me to find a power place. Listen to your spirit. Drive around, or go for walks around your home until you find a place that speaks to you. Let the power of the earth fill you with love.

Day 174

Black Sun

We see the sun with our physical eyes, but it isn't real. When we focus on the tonal or on physical reality, we seldom see the spirit or *Nagual*. "The mists thinned and in the distance the woman could see beauty beyond her wildest imaginings." It is the spirit that gives all things life. It is the black sun that is real.

The force of creation lives in the spaces between what we see. The black sun gives light to physical reality.

Meditate on the idea of the black sun; feel it, touch it, sense it, and let it teach you.

Day 175

Preparation: A Meditation

Imagine yourself sitting down to meditate. Your mind immediately becomes still and your body settles into a deep state of peace and relaxation. You sit quietly and feel your heart fill with love. You connect with your innate wisdom and goodness. It has become easy and effortless.

Breathe deeply, grateful for the ease, for the sense of connection, and for this time to sit and relax. You look forward to meditating and smile at how hard you used to make it. Give thanks for the quiet, the love, the peace, and your ability to meditate.

Day 176

Elements

Earth, air, water, and fire are the elements we traditionally call upon before a ceremony. Think about the four elements. Which one most speaks to your heart? Which is your favorite? Which of the elements speaks to you the least?

Take a deep breath and call upon the elements one by one. Feel them, connect with them, and listen to them. Ask them to guide you and teach you.

Then take another deep breath and sit quietly with the elements.

DAY 177

Fire

Fire symbolizes the energy of transformation. Build a fire in your fireplace or an outdoor firepit, or light a candle and watch its flame. Let the flames speak to you. Open your heart so you can feel the energy of the fire.

You can use fire in many ways. Write cathartic letters or prayers on paper and burn them. Let the wind carry away the ashes. Let yourself connect with the element of fire.

Day 178

Wind

Stand where you can feel the wind on your body. Close your eyes and feel it caress you. Feel it move your clothes and hair. Stand in silence and connect with the wind. Now let the wind blow through your body. Imagine the wind blowing through your mind, and watch it blow away your fear-based, limiting thoughts.

Fully experience the wind: listen to it, embrace it, and let your consciousness flow with it. Imagine where the air you just inhaled has been. Perhaps it was Buddha's last breath or the first breath Jesus took. The wind itself is invisible, but its effects are very evident. Think about how wind can become your teacher.

DAY 179

The Sun

Stand outside and feel the warmth of the sun on your face. Close your eyes and turn your face directly into its heat. Breathe in the sunlight. Take it into your heart; let it warm you and fill you. Spend five minutes breathing in the sun.

Now imagine the sunlight going right through you. Feel the rays of the sun flowing through your body, moving effortless through you and around you. What can the sun teach you?

Day 180

Swimming: A Meditation

The sun is warm and the water invites you. You wade along the shore feeling totally peaceful. Then you see the whales surface and hear their song. It vibrates through your body, calling you, urging you on. Dive into the water, swimming effortlessly toward them.

A whale surfaces beside you. You look into her eye and a tear trickles down your check. You've never been so deeply moved. You feel an almost overwhelming love. Your heart beats faster as you swim alongside her.

You become one with the whale. See the ocean as your home, giving you food and comfort, always there, surrounding you with love. The sunlight dances through the water and lights your way. Your freedom and joy are limitless. The ocean seems endless and so full of life.

Take a deep breath and once again find yourself swimming alongside the whale. She looks at you a bit longer before she swims off to be with her calf. As you swim back to the shore, give thanks for the gift.

Day 181

Seasons

What is your favorite season? How do you celebrate the seasons? Do you notice the subtle changes in light, day by day? What time of year do you have the most energy? Are there seasons that make you want to stay at home? What else do you notice? Connect with the rhythm of the earth. "The woman was no longer listening. Her attention was fully hooked by her five senses." Engage your senses and notice how the seasons affect you.

Day 182

Time

Time is fluid. The only moment that exists is the present moment. When we feel bored, time seems to go very slowly, yet when we enjoy ourselves, time goes very quickly. We can consciously change our experience of time and even learn to bend it. The next time you think you are going to be late, clearly picture yourself arriving a few minutes early, and see what happens. I've been known to get someplace in a few minutes when it should take at least half an hour. Play with time, let it become your friend.

"... bit by bit you will remember that physical reality is an illusion," the woman heard. "One day you will realize that reality lies beyond what your eyes see, that reality lives in the land of the mists."

Day 183

Consciousness

We often think that the mind and consciousness are two separate entities, but they are one. Today, become aware of your consciousness as separate from your mind.

Where does your consciousness reside most of the time? Play with moving it around in your body. Do you feel your consciousness in your heart? Your stomach? Under what circumstances does your consciousness move to a different place? Be conscious of your consciousness.

Day 184

Scents

Our sense of smell can be a very powerful emotional trigger. You can use scents to help you relax or to wake up. We often associate coffee with morning. Peppermint enhances memory, and lavender is good for healing.

Find a scented candle or incense that you enjoy and light it before you meditate. Eventually it will act as a reminder to your mind that it is time to be quiet.

Play with scents. Notice what various scents do for your body and your emotional state. If you wear a particular perfume or cologne, try a totally new scent. How does the new scent make you feel? Act? What scents take you back in time? Think about the scents you are currently establishing memories for.

Day 185

Trees

Stand next to a tree and lean against its trunk. Call upon the elements and the directions. Ask them for their guidance and protection. Ask the tree's permission to become one with it and then open your heart. As you lean against the tree, imagine its sap rising up through you. After a few minutes you may become aware of a gentle rocking in your body. When the rocking stops, thank the tree, the elements, and the directions.

Notice how you feel afterward.

Day 186

Your Toes

When you feel confused or lost, look down at your toes. Imagine that they root you to the ground. Remember that you are right here, right now, in this present moment. Whatever is happening is just the way it is.

day 187

Mirror

In a darkened room, sit in front of a large mirror. Light a candle and watch your reflection. With a soft focus notice the shadows in the room. Breathe deeply, imagine yourself connecting with a deep part of your divinity, and watch the shadows change. Spend at least fifteen minutes in front of the mirror. Surround yourself with love and be with the experience.

day 188

Frame of Reference

Hold your hands before your face with your thumbs and fingers together to form a box. Close one eye and look through the box. Scan the room and notice how you can only see a small portion of the room at one time. You have just limited your frame of reference. If you make the opening between your fingers small enough, you won't even be able to identify what you are looking at. Now lower your hands and look at the room with no limits.

Most of us look at life through a very tiny opening. What would happen if we suddenly enlarged that opening? Think of death—how would death look if you could see the big picture?

Day 189

Looking

Look around your room. What catches your attention? What about it did your mind find fascinating? Have a dialogue with it. What does it have to say? What do you want to say to it? What does it represent to you? Does it engender love or fear?

Now look around the room again. Consciously decide to focus your attention on one thing in the room. Have the same dialogue with that thing and observe any thoughts or feeling you have.

DAY 190

Healing: A Meditation

See yourself walking toward an ancient temple. It shimmers and almost appears translucent. You move slowly up the path, pausing to greet your fellow travelers. At the entrance you are welcomed by two beautiful beings of light. They take your hands and lead you to the inner sanctum of the temple. They remove your shoes and clothing, anoint you with the finest oils, and dress you in a white robe.

The beings lead you toward an altar that stands in the very center of the temple. As you approach, feel yourself float upward and find yourself lying on the altar. You feel a warmth surge through your body. Take a deep breath and feel all your cares and concerns fall away. You look up into the eyes of the being standing near the head of the altar and see love and acceptance. As you continue to look into that being's eyes, feel a healing take place deep within your core.

You are home at last.

DAY 191

Staying in Balance

It is so easy to get off balance. When we align ourselves with our small self, we can easily swing between emotional highs and lows and cover our fear with anger.

But when we connect with our center or essence, we feel balanced, at ease with life, and more open and loving. Gently rock back and forth inside yourself until you feel completely balanced. Take a few deep breaths and imagine yourself finding that place of balance within. The woman "became aware of herself for the first time. She looked at the mists swirling around her and she knew she was everywhere and nowhere. She was everyone and no one."

Remember to return to your balanced center often as you move through your day.

DAY 192

Feeling Safe

How often do you make choices based on your desire to feel safe? One of the most important questions I ever answered for myself is, "Is this a safe universe or a hostile one?" When you align yourself with your mind, the answer is "a hostile one," but as you learn to connect with your divinity, you realize you are always safe.

Today whenever you are feeling unsure or fearful, take a few deep breaths and connect with your spiritual essence. Feel safe.

DAY 193

Small Self

My small self is very fear based. When I am aligned with that part of myself, I feel reactive and disconnected. My response is to be defensive. But as long as I hid my small self, I could not heal that part of me. Once I embraced her, I could use her gifts and minimize the chaos she created.

Take some time to embrace and listen to your small self. Acknowledge that side of yourself, and begin to expose the hidden gifts there.

DAY 194

Doing Nothing

Take an hour today and do absolutely nothing. Don't read or watch TV or listen to music—just sit and do nothing. Find a comfortable place, sit quietly, and allow yourself to enjoy being in the moment. Notice your resistance to doing this, if you have any. Notice how often you find yourself lost in thought or ruminating on something you need to do.

Most of us have mastered the skill of doing. Very few of us ever master the skill of being. We learn by practicing, so practice doing nothing. Notice how you feel about nothing. Is it even possible to do nothing?

Day 195

Keep on Keeping On

If we want to transform our lives we have to keep practicing new behaviors. Occasionally, the best we can do is to keep on keeping on. Don't give up five minutes before the miracle occurs. The most important time to keep going is when you really don't want to. Your freedom always lies in the opposite direction to where you think you ought to go.

Day 196

Putting on the Energy Of . . .

Imagine putting on a big overcoat. Feel its weight on your body, smell the fabric, and snuggle into its warmth. That was easy wasn't it?

Now imagine putting on the energy of abundance, of peace of mind, of love, or of personal freedom. We are always putting on the energy of something—why not consciously decide to put on the energy of something wonderful?

chapter 8

Heaven on Earth

The Grandmother and the children sat at the edge of a stand of tall pine trees. She looked out over the land.

"We are the land's caretakers and we must always plant more than we use. If you cut down a tree, you must plant at least two more. Mother Earth will always provide for us, but in thanks for her love we must also care for her just as we care for one another.

"When we share with each other, there is always more than enough, yet when we are afraid to share, there is never enough.

"In one village the people had learned to live in gratitude, generosity, and love. They ate together at a huge table full of food. The bowls were always full and overflowing. Everyone had spoons with long handles attached to their arms. They all laughed and joyously fed one another.

"In another village the people lived in fear. They, too, had spoons with long handles attached to their arms, but they couldn't reach their own mouths. When they tried to feed themselves, the food fell uselessly to the table. Although their bowls overflowed, they were all starving to death.

"We can live in heaven or hell. Where we live depends on what we tell ourselves. If we live in fear, we will live in hell. If we remember the power of love, we can live in heaven.

"Look at your world. What do you see? Are you eager to be an adult, or are you enjoying being a child? Do you wish you lived in another village, or are you grateful for the home you have?

"If you listen to your mind's endless list of wants, you will never be happy. Learn to listen to your heart and you will always find joy. Let your heart guide your choices.

"Let nature teach you how to quiet your mind. Listen to the wind; sit by a stream and listen to the water or watch the light move on its surface. Watch the clouds. Sit close to a tree and let its spirit teach you. Pay attention to your senses. Feel the magic of life as it flows through your body, and your mind will grow still. Feel, taste, touch, smell, and see. Be in the moment rather than thinking about being there.

"Let nature show you the silence of your mind. Be still and watch the love grow. In the silence we see that heaven lives in our hearts and in our minds. You don't have to go anywhere to find heaven. It is always just a thought away."

DAY 197

Seeing

When I say to see the energy, most people focus on visual cues. One of our tasks is to discover how we see and to deepen our ability to see in our own way, as well as to expand our definition of *seeing*.

Find an object that attracts you—a blade of grass, a flower, a rock, a piece of jewelry, or any object that catches your attention.

Set aside at least half an hour when you won't be disturbed. Sit with the object—look at it, smell it, feel it. Use your senses to "see" it. Go through your five senses and experience the object. Then gently close your eyes and be with the object. Allow yourself to sense its presence. How do you know it is there? How do you feel in its presence? Allow yourself to "see" the object and allow yourself to be seen.

Let go of your mind's definition of seeing and see what you see. Learn how you see. "You don't have to go anywhere to find heaven," the Grandmother said. "It is always just a thought away."

day 198

Physical Energy

What we perceive as physical energy is an illusion. A physical object is mostly space, yet we see it as solid. Our senses tell us physicality is real, but is it? Is this world anything but an illusion? What in this physical world is permanent? We are here for only an instant. Where will your body be in a hundred years?

How do you know how to interpret the marks on this page? How much of your attention do you focus on physicality? What is beyond the limits of this page? Can you feel my words, or are you just reading them? It's so easy to get trapped in our minds. Notice what you feel as you read these words. Take a deep breath and feel rather than simply thinking about what you are reading.

day 199

Heaven or Hell

Heaven and hell both exist in our minds. Where you spend your time depends on what you tell yourself about life. A woman whose granddaughter had just died contacted me. She was devastated and wanted to know how she could possibly live with her grief. I suggested she allow for the possibility that we can continue to have a relationship with people after they die.

A few days later I received a joyful note saying her granddaughter's spirit had come to her several times and told her it was her time to shine. The woman wasn't sure what that referred to, but the contact transformed her grief and changed her whole perspective toward life and death.

Her granddaughter was still dead, but the woman's experience of her loss became entirely different. We always have the choice to be in heaven or hell depending on what we tell ourselves.

Day 200

Gaining Energy

What can you do to gain energy? What thoughts and feelings are expansive for you? What activities invigorate you? Which foods give you a quick boost and which ones sustain you? How often do you check your energy level before deciding what to do?

Monitor your energy for a day. Try to keep track of what affects your energy.

DAY 201

Hopelessness

Being without hope is often a powerful state. When we have hope, we focus on a future event. When we are without hope, we can choose to make the best out of the present moment.

Whenever you feel hopeless ask yourself, "What can I tell myself right now to feel at peace? What choice can I make right now from a place of love?" Hopelessness is caused by what we tell ourselves about events, not the events themselves.

"Learn to listen to your heart and you will always find joy. Let your heart guide your choices."

DaY 202

Big Goblins: A Meditation

Imagine yourself lying in bed. You know there is a whole family of big goblins living beneath it. Take a few deep breaths and fill yourself with love. You notice that the room grows brighter as you breathe in love and exhale anything unlike love. Sit up knowing you are surrounded by love and feeling a profound connection to your higher self.

Take a few more deep breaths and invite the goblins to come out and talk to you. As the goblins step into the circle of light, you smile. They smile in return and your fear completely goes away. You realize the goblins are just beings of light who have also forgotten how to find their way home.

You talk with one another about your fears, your journeys, your dreams, and your paths. The goblins you used to fear become companions on your journey home.

Day 203

Happiness

What do you tell yourself that makes you happy? What if you expanded your definition of happiness to include things that normally disturb you?

Think of something that makes you happy. You might picture your favorite pet, a beautiful sunrise, or a wonderful event. Once you feel happy let the image go and just feel the emotion.

Let the happiness build and grow in your body. How do you experience happiness in your body? Where do you feel it? During the day, practice creating the feelings you most associate with happiness in your body. Practice until you can generate the feeling of happiness at will. The next time you find yourself afraid, generate the feeling of happiness and then invite the fear to join you. See how that affects your perspective.

DAY 204

Emotions as Energy

We experience true freedom when we live our lives from our spirits instead of from our minds. As we learn to do so, we begin to experience this world as a vast energy system. We learn to feel the energy—not think about it or have emotions about it but to simply feel it. Our minds love to tell stories about our feelings.

As we retrain our minds, it is helpful to learn how to move into the energy of love. Take a deep breath and think about the energy of love; fill your entire body with that feeling. Now think about fear and feel that energy fully. When we allow ourselves to simply be angry or afraid rather than think about those emotions, we can learn to just change gears.

Day 205

Rules

At one point in your life you made up rules to help you make sense of the chaos around you. We all do. Through the eyes of a child, you looked at the world and created rules about how things worked; now you continue to live with these rules.

How many rules do you think you have? How many are based on false assumptions? Today, notice the rules you apply to yourself, to your world, and to the events that occur during the day. How many times do your rules tell you the right thing to do?

When you are fully present in the moment, you don't need rules to tell you how to act. As long as you remain unaware of your rules, you limit your choice-making capacity. Connect with your spirit and make your choices in the moment.

Day 206

The Energy of Death

We celebrate a birth; why don't we celebrate death as well? Death is a natural part of life. When we die in body, we are reborn in spirit.

Death is an incredible teacher. The first time I encountered the energy of death, I was standing on the beach. I had no idea what the energy was, but my body recognized it and immediately started to shake uncontrollably. I spent many weeks thinking about and playing with that energy until we became friends. The energy of death is very powerful, loving, and gentle. It is nothing to fear; death is simply another energy shift. What are your thoughts about death? How do you feel about death? Sit quietly, breathe deeply, and imagine your body dying.

Go into nature and notice the natural cycle of birth and death. Call upon the energy of death. Spend some time with it and get to know it. Let go of your preconceived ideas and just feel the energy of death. Let it teach you, embrace your fear, and open your heart to its energy. Once you get to know it, you will never have to fear death again.

DAY 207

Letting Go of the Past: A Meditation

You've been walking for a very long time and you feel tired, hungry, and thirsty. The straps from your pack cut into your shoulders. Although your pack is very heavy, you are afraid to put it down.

You come upon a town and in its center you discover a well. An old woman hands you a tin cup full of cool water. You drink, hand the cup back to her, and are very grateful when she gives you another. You lean against the well and drink slowly. You thank her then find a shady spot to sit and rest. As you look around, you see many other travelers just like you. They all carry heavy packs and look tired and hungry. They sit in stark contrast to the townspeople, who seem very happy.

The old woman approaches you and asks if you've come for the ceremony. Your look of confusion is enough to answer her question. She smiles knowingly, says she is glad you have come, and walks off. You find yourself getting very sleepy.

When you awaken the scene has changed. A huge bonfire burns where the well had stood. You watch as the other travelers walk to the fire, one by one, and throw their packs into it. You wonder why they would do that. Then you see their faces. They look happy and free.

The old woman stands beside you and whispers in your ear, "Your pack is full of pain from the past—all of your limiting thoughts, agreements, assumptions, and beliefs."

She steps aside and at first you hesitate; you're uncertain. Some people stand defiantly holding onto their packs. Some walk away, proudly replacing their packs on their backs. You wait for a moment and then you run to the fire. You open your pack and begin throwing things into the flames. Finally, with a huge sigh of relief, you throw in your empty pack. You watch as it's consumed and you rejoice.

day 208

Changing Your Energy

Since we are beings of energy, all change is energetic. Think of something you successfully changed in the past. How did you feel before and after the change? Think of something that felt very limiting in your life. When you released that limitation, how did you feel?

When we change in some way, we shift our energy field. When we go back to an old behavior, our energy field has gone back to a familiar pattern. If you don't get along with your boss, you will probably have problems with your next boss, as well—unless you change your beliefs about bosses.

Today notice the energy with which you approach the events in your day. When you interact with your boss, does your energy feel limiting or expansive? What events of the day expand your energy? How can you harness that expansiveness to change the things that make your energy feel limiting?

DaY 209

Tug of War

In order to play tug of war someone has to pull on each end of the rope. Life gives us many opportunities to play tug of war. If you want to experience peace instead of war, don't pull—instead let go of your end of the rope. When you learn to embrace everything in your life, the quality of your life will improve drastically and your ability to change will increase as well.

Today whenever you feel like fighting with someone or something, consciously drop your end of the rope. "Live," as the Grandmother advised, "in gratitude and generosity, and love."

DAY 210

Managing Energy

At all times, our energy is either expanding or contracting. We are either leaking energy or gaining energy. Neither is right or wrong. When I perform a ceremony, I gain a great deal of energy. I find it useful to dissipate some of it if I want to sleep that night. Since I hold many of my ceremonies on the beach, I stand in the surf, and let the energy flow back into the earth. I can also stand in the ocean to gain energy. It depends on my intent.

Observe your energy states. Observe what you do to build energy and what you do to dissipate energy. Play with gaining and losing energy so you can draw on it or shed it at will.

DAY 211

Process

A process has a beginning, middle, and end.

Define what *process* means to you, how you feel about it, and how much you understand your relationship to it. Are you comfortable with waiting for a process to unfold? How does process operate in your life?

What is your process with regard to relationships, change, life, death, love, clarity, understanding, surrender, your divinity, or acceptance? As you think through these, consider how you can use process to work through problems or embrace joyful moments.

DaY 212

Doing the Dishes

I used to hate doing the dishes and would put them off until I absolutely had to. Then one day I realized I love taking long, hot bubble baths and that washing the dishes is nothing more than giving my hands a bath. Ever since then I love doing the dishes.

What do you hate to do that you could learn to love instead? Sometimes just changing your perception slightly can make an experience totally different.

DAY 213

The Gift: A Meditation

You awaken with a deep sense of anticipation. Today is the day, the day you can finally open the gift. You race downstairs and find it waiting for you in the middle of the floor, beautifully wrapped. The paper looks magnificent, and the ribbons weave together in intricate patterns. You find yourself lost in the ancient symbols you discover in them. You think about how you can apply the symbols to your life until your stomach growls, making you realize you've been playing with the ribbons for hours. You rip them off and again notice the paper. As you look closer, you see hundreds of words hidden in the patterns. The stories fascinate you. The words go on and on. Several hours later you have barely finished reading one side of the package.

The gift. You remember the gift is inside the package. You rip off the paper and notice the beauty of the box. For a moment you are tempted to stop and explore the box. You smile at yourself and open the gift. You look inside and see yourself, and you finally remember you were the gift all along.

DAY 214

Communicating with the Elements

I used to hate the wind until I learned to listen to it. Now the wind works with me. Whenever I perform a ceremony the wind responds.

Spend some time in nature. What is the harm of a few raindrops falling on you? What falls more softly than a blanket of snow? The elements will speak to you if you take the time to listen. Consciously focus on each element until you develop a relationship with it. Practice calling up each of the elements until you can feel them respond to you.

DAY 215

Interdependence

At one extreme there is independence and at the other is codependence. Imagine yourself interconnected to everyone and everything. We are all one. We are all interdependent.

Today, experience your connectedness rather than focusing on your sense of separation. As you go about the day, embrace that connectedness. When you and someone you care about head your separate ways for the day, focus on what connects you, not what draws you apart. As you go through the day, think about what connects you to the people you encounter, and how your activities fit into your life as a whole. Experiment with the feeling of interdependence.

Day 216

No Limits

Imagine living without limits. How freeing that would feel. Words like *expansive, light, joyous,* and *fluid* come to mind for me. What would it mean to you to be limitless? We are often painfully aware of our limitations. Do you allow yourself to experience being limitless in any areas of your life?

Imagine what your life would be like if you had absolutely no limitations. In what areas of your life are you willing and able to release your limitations? Spend some time today just imagining being limitless.

Day 217

Fluidity

Water flows easily and effortlessly. Yet its effortless motion has the strength to create the Grand Canyon. How can anything that is so fluid be so powerful?

How could you use the concept of fluidity in your life? What would happen if you embraced the idea of simply going with the flow of life? What Grand Canyon could you create? Play with being fluid today. "Feel the magic of life as it flows though your body, and your mind will grow still."

day 218

Creating Your Sanctuary: A Meditation

Imagine a tiny "you" standing in front of yourself. You walk toward an opening right in the middle of your forehead, leap into space, and find yourself flying down toward the very center of your being. The ride is exhilarating. You laugh with joy.

At the center of your being is a very special place: your sanctuary. It is a place of peace, full of wisdom, where you can connect with yourself, recharge your spirit, and bask in the love.

Take some time now and create your sanctuary. It can be a place or simply a feeling. Decorate it. Fill it with whatever pleases you—mountains and streams, lots of things, or nothing at all.

DAY 219

Altars

An altar is a wonderful addition to any space, a symbol of something special and important. An altar can be elaborate or simply a corner of your desk. You can make a portable altar by gathering some favorite objects and a unique piece of cloth in a pouch.

Create an altar in your home. Make it as elaborate or simple as you like. Use a corner of a dresser if you don't have enough room for a completely separate space. Care for your altar with love, and watch the energy of your altar grow.

Day 220

Supreme Being

Whatever you choose to call your supreme being—the Great Spirit, God, Goddess, the Creator, all there is, or simply energy—set your intent to have a personal relationship with it.

Volumes can be written about the experience. My experience of the energy has changed over the years as I cleared out my filter system. As soon as I describe the energy, I limit it. I could describe it as totally expansive, limitless, accepting, emotionally neutral, loving, powerful, gentle, and completely nonjudgmental. It doesn't care what I do or don't do. Whatever I ask for, it replies, "Sure, if that is what you truly want." But that is my experience. This path will allow you to have a direct experience for yourself, not one simply described to you by someone else. Set your intent, ask for the willingness to develop that relationship, and eventually you will.

DAY 221

Music

Sit and listen to several pieces of music. Close your eyes, allow yourself to feel each piece, even listen to the spaces between the sounds. Let the music fill you. What does the sound feel like in your body? Do you see colors? Notice your breath as you listen to the music.

As you go about your day, listen to the melodies of life. Listen without judgment to the sounds that annoy you. Listen to the rhythms of the noises in your world. Listen to the music of your life.

DAY 222

Moving into the Energy

Imagine the energy of abundance. How does it feel? How does your body react to that energy? Think about the energy of scarcity. How does that feel?

Practice switching from one energy state to another. What does that feel like? The next time you need to make a choice, move into the energy of joy. See how that energy affects your choice.

Day 223

How Do You Know?

How do you know what you know? How do you know that you know what you know? When did you know it? How do you process knowing?

We continually learn. But if you are currently in a formal program of study, as you acquire knowledge, think about the process as you move from not knowing to knowing. When do you begin to feel differently?

DQY 224

Breath

Take some deep breaths. Focus your attention on your breathing. Does your breath come easy or hard, shallow or deep? Is your chest tight, or are you breathing deep into your stomach? Notice where you feel your breath in your body.

Close your eyes and take ten slow, deep breaths. Do you notice a difference in how you feel? Today pause frequently during the day and take at least five deep breaths. Notice how you feel at the end of the day. Do you feel different than you did the day before when you didn't concentrate on breathing deeply?

chapter 9

What Would Love Do?

"Grandmother, were you always a storyteller?"

"No my child. Once I was a little girl just like you. I liked to play and laugh, but I always felt a connection to the spirit. One day, many moons ago, a wolf came into my life and changed everything.

"It had been a long, cold winter. I couldn't sleep one night, and as I wandered through the village I came upon a wolf. Before I had a chance to run away, I noticed that he had injured his paw. I knew I should fear him, but deep in my being a question arose: 'What would love do?' In that moment I knew the wolf was a gift; I reached out and patted his head. I told him I would return with help. A trusting friend helped me carry the wolf into my home.

"The wolf's eyes filled with gratitude as we laid him on a blanket. I cleaned his wound and gave him a bowl of broth made with a scrap of meat. He drank the broth, and as soon as he had finished, he fell asleep.

"I was tired so I laid down next to the wolf. His presence was comforting, and I quickly fell into a deep sleep. Suddenly I found myself standing before the ancient ones and the wolf stood beside me. I was frightened at first. I felt very humble and small.

"The ancient ones smiled and said to me, 'We are very proud of you, little one. You reached out in love. You set aside your fear and saved this being's life. People have too long worked alone. They have come to believe that they are superior to the earth and the other animals. But you are all one, my child.'

"For years I had felt this way. I had listened to the whisperings of love but I tried to close my heart to the message. I was afraid. The other children often made fun of me for my sensitivity. Hearing the truth gave me the courage to speak to the ancient ones.

"'When I try to tell others that the animals talk to me, they just laugh,' I said. 'I hear the spirits of the land and of all its creatures. The earth is sacred; we must love it and treat everything in it with love.'

"The ancient ones nodded and replied, 'That is why you are here little one. You are here to take a message back to your elders. You will teach with your stories. You will remind others that all of life is sacred and that you are meant to live in harmony. You must teach others to treat everyone and everything with dignity and respect.

Humankind must learn to act in love, not with fear, anger, hatred, or greed. People must work together, in that way they will again find their way home.'

"'But how will I get the people to listen?' I asked.

"'Trust little one,' the ancient ones said, 'the story of how you tamed the wolf is already spreading. The wolf is a feared creature, yet you healed this one and saved its life. You slept beside him with no fear for your own safety. The people now know you are special.'

"When I awoke in the morning I could hear people outside, talking. When I stepped out of my dwelling, the wolf stood beside me. A murmur went through the crowd. I loved that wolf and he was with me for many years. I will enjoy meeting him again when my job here is done.

"When I spoke, my voice had changed and people listened. I was not yet ready to be a storyteller, but people did pay attention when I spoke of my dreams.

"It is time for sleep. Remember your dreams, little ones. You never know who will visit you. Sweet dreams."

The Grandmother's heart was full of joy as she watched her young charges wander off to their homes. Love is such a wonderful gift when it's freely given.

DAY 225

Can't Get There Until You Get There

You can't resolve an issue until you resolve an issue. You can't see life from a spiritual perspective until you can see it from a spiritual perspective. If you feel like a victim in a certain area of your life, feel it. Really allow yourself to discover how small and helpless you feel. Become aware of all your limiting thoughts, and don't judge them until you are ready to let them go.

You can't change something until you are ready to change it. Admitting to yourself that you're not ready doesn't mean you do nothing. Admitting you're not ready allows you the freedom to take any action necessary to become willing to change.

You can't see what's on the other side of the mountain until you get to the top of the mountain. Sitting by the side of the trail fuming won't get you to the top one moment sooner, but putting one foot in front of the other will. Start moving your feet and enjoy the journey.

Day 226

Suffering Is Optional

Pain is part of life. Relationships will end and close friends will die. Such loss is painful but suffering is optional. Emotions come and go easily if we let them. We can feel sadness in one moment and in the next moment joy. Suffering occurs only when we continue to hold on to a thought or feeling. If we stay in the moment, we may experience pain, but it will pass and the next moment will arrive.

Even when we feel physical pain, if we stay in the moment we don't have to suffer. We simply experience pain in the moment. Suffering is an option we can let go of anytime we want. But we have to be willing to let it go. We can do that by changing what we tell ourselves about the present moment.

DAY 227

Hurting or Healing

Anything, including our thoughts or actions, can hurt or heal us. It all depends upon our motives. I once had a student who judged herself harshly all the time. It became evident to me that her underlying intent was to punish herself. Once she saw that, too, she learned to stop hurting herself.

Observe what you do with the information you receive. Do you use it to judge yourself? Do you feel you should have "it" by now? Are you using that information to help yourself grow? The more we know, the easier it is for us to prove that there is something "wrong" with us. If you are gentle and loving with yourself, you are more likely to use these tools for healing rather than hurting yourself.

Day 228

Shadow Self

We all have what we could perceive as a light side and a dark side. Our dark side, or shadow self, stores the behaviors, thoughts, feelings, and beliefs that we don't like, that we hide from others.

By hiding our shadow self we disconnect from a large part of who we are. We lose access to many valuable gifts and talents. For instance, if you delegate your anger to your shadow self, you may find it difficult to be assertive. Reconnecting with our divinity is a process of integration that includes embracing the shadow.

Define your shadow self. What are the darkest parts of your being that you keep hidden, sometimes even from yourself?

DAY 229

Wrapping Yourself in Love

Before you go to sleep at night, imagine wrapping yourself in a blanket of love. Feel it as you pull it around yourself; feel it filling your heart and your mind. When you wake up in the morning, notice how it feels to have slept surrounded by love. "I was tired so I laid down next to the wolf. His presence was comforting, and I quietly fell into a deep sleep," the Grandmother said in her story about the wounded wolf.

Day 230

The Hot Air Balloon: A Meditation

You are standing on the top of a hill. Off in the distance you see a beautiful hot air balloon drifting along. You see that it is about to land on the next hill, and you begin to race toward it. The basket appears empty. As it settles down you move a little closer. When you look deep into the basket, you discover an unusual creature with large eyes and long, long arms. Its expression is very sweet and loving. It reaches out and gently caresses your face. With an ancient voice, it tells you to put all your emotional pain, worries, and cares into the basket. It offers to take care of them for you, and you know it is so.

The creature hands you a pen and paper and tells you to write it all down. You start writing furiously. You don't want to leave out a thing. The creature watches you lovingly, patiently waiting for you to finish. When you stop writing, it takes the paper from you, places its hands on your head and your heart, and whispers a prayer.

The hot air balloon slowly begins to rise. You feel incredibly free and light, just like the balloon. You look up and see a small, beautifully wrapped package floating toward you. Its small card says, "This is a blessing just for you."

DαY 231

Everything Is a Gift

When we view everything as a gift, we can unwrap the package, uncover another piece of our filter system, and release it. If we fight the experience, we are unlikely to see our filters and more likely to strengthen our resolve to hold on to limiting beliefs.

Track your thoughts and feelings as you view everything as a gift. See what you learn about your filter system.

Day 232

Wanting

Everything in your life is there because you want it there. Everything that isn't in your life isn't there because you don't want it there. That's just the nature of physical reality. Wanting and having are two very different energy states.

Think about it. How does it feel in your body when you want something? How does it feel when you already have something? The two feel very different.

When you project the energy of wanting, you actually push the very thing you want away. With the energy of having you attract it. Play with the energy of wanting and the energy of having. Practice shifting from one energy state to the other and see what happens. If you really want to have something in your life, feel yourself having it and you will; stay with wanting it and you may continue wanting it forever.

DAY 233

How Does Your Mind Think?

Have you ever wondered how your mind thinks? Our emotions are stored in what is called the limbic brain. Psychobiologists are discovering fascinating things about our three levels of consciousness and the role of the limbic brain in our thought processes. The ancient ones knew that if we were to achieve personal freedom, we would need to separate our emotions from our actions. Our minds don't deal with facts. They deal with an emotional interpretation of the facts. We see life as we think it is rather than how it really is.

Notice today how many things in life you are emotionally neutral about.

DaY 234

Discernment

When I first started to get in touch with my inner wisdom, I had a hard time distinguishing my mind from my spirit. Eventually I noticed that my spirit never gave me a sales pitch. It gently and lovingly said, "Look at the rainbow." My mind, on the other hand, nagged me to hurry up and look at the rainbow, or it said I had too many things to do to stop and look. Sometimes it judged the rainbow and how often I had seen others, or it said that I spent too much time looking at rainbows and not enough time doing other things. My mind will try to sell me on an idea, give me all the pros and cons, and generally keep me so busy that by the time I actually look, the rainbow is long gone.

Our shadow self, our spirit, our mind, and all the parts of our being have voices. Each one is slightly different. Just as you can discern the differences between the voices of your friends, you can learn to discern your inner voices. The voice of my mind is often judgmental and harsh, while my spirit's voice is more full of gentle curiosity.

DAY 235

Perspective

There is no such thing as reality. Everything is based on our perspective about reality. If we change our perspective, what we think of as reality changes as well. There are no absolutes except that there are absolutely no absolutes—and even that isn't absolute.

Pause during the course of the day and ask of a given situation, "How could I see this differently?" Even if you like what you see, try to see it differently. Observe any attachment you have to seeing things positively or resistance you might have to seeing things negatively.

DaY 236

Floating: A Meditation

The water in the tidal pool is warm and inviting, a rich shade of turquoise. You take a deep breath, immerse yourself in the water, and your body immediately begins to float. The water is so buoyant it supports your body with ease. You feel as if you are floating in a sea of love.

Lie back and watch the clouds float by. The water gently laps at the edges of the pool, soothing your mind and your spirit. Your breathing slows and you feel the energy of life all about you in the water. Breathe in the love; breathe in the peace. Relax and surrender, trusting that the water will safely support you.

DAY 237

Should

When I lived in Nantucket, I loved taking the ferry home from the mainland. You could always identify the tourists; they stood at the back of the boat feeding the seagulls until the inevitable happened. The local shops sold T-shirts that looked like they were covered with seagull shit. In big letters the T-shirts proclaimed, "Don't Shit On Me!" I've played with the idea of creating a T-shirt that reads: "Don't Should on Me!"

Should is one of our small self's favorite words: "I should have . . ." or "I should do . . ." or "You should . . ." *Should* doesn't empower us; it is a subtle form of judgment. Whenever my mind starts telling me what I should do, I think of that T-shirt and remind myself not to should on myself. Observe your use of the word *should*. Ask yourself, do you really want to spend so much time on your small self?

Day 238

Control

What role does control play in your life? Do you need to feel in control in order to feel safe? Can you really control anything other than your responses? Can you even control them?

What does the need to be in control feel like? What does being controlled feel like? Is the energy of control expansive or limiting? How much energy do you exert each day on the idea of control?

DAY 239

Traffic

Traffic can be a petty tyrant for many people, or it can be a gift. The next time you find yourself in traffic, notice your inner dialogue; notice your judgments, fears, and reactions. We often use phrases like "stuck in traffic," "tied up in traffic," or "caught in a traffic jam."

While you are sitting in traffic you can send love to the people around you, mentally recite a gratitude list, or be mindfully in the moment. How can you use sitting in traffic to help you achieve personal freedom?

Day 240

Responsibility

Being responsible and being at fault are very different. Often when we feel responsible, what we are really doing is blaming ourselves for not doing something right or perfectly. We feel at fault.

Responsibility is simply your ability to respond to a situation. Notice your thoughts and responses to the idea of being responsible for your experience of reality. Write definitions of *fault* and *responsibility*. Start to learn not to confuse one with the other.

DAY 241

Mind Candy

What would you most like to change about your life? Do you spend a great deal of time trying to understand this issue? Will an understanding of what you'd like to change really help set you free, or is it just something that keeps your mind busy? Is it just mind candy?

Even if you thoroughly understand an issue, nothing will change unless you make different choices. Instead of asking why you want to make this change or why this issue is so predominant in your life, try asking these questions: "How else can I see this issue?" or "What other choice can I make right now?" or "What would love do?" What concrete actions can you take today to make this change? Make a list of the things you can do to change and do at least one every day.

DAY 242

Limitless: A Meditation

You are standing at the edge of infinity. It stretches out for an eternity in every direction. Let yourself breathe in the expansiveness. Imagine yourself going on without end, forever and ever. Feel infinity as it flows through you. Feel eternity as it embraces you. Take a few deep breaths and allow yourself to be with that energy.

You are a limitless being of light. You are infinite and eternal. You are one with the universe. You are limitless. Allow those thoughts to resonate in your being.

DAY 243

Who Are You?

Our awareness of ourselves and of life has many levels. I remember many years ago being in the shower and asking myself, "Who am I?" Ruminating on that question gave me an awareness that sent my life in a totally new direction.

New information is constantly altering your awareness. Who are you? Where can answering that question take you? What are you aware of and how are you aware of it? Play with the idea of awareness and see where it takes you.

DAY 244

Being Consistent

People are consistent. If someone lies to everyone else, he will also likely lie to you. If we look honestly at ourselves, we must concede that we know how to be consistent. People don't do things to us, they just do what they do; sometimes we happen to be there.

Since we already know how to be consistent, we can use that knowledge in several ways. We can experience realistic expectations about people, including ourselves. Once we realize people are consistent, we won't feel disappointed when a friend who has a hard time with honesty doesn't tell us when she is upset. We expect such people to communicate indirectly and act accordingly.

We can also use our ability to be consistent to assist us in our growth. We can consistently do things that help us change. We can meditate or journal or be mindful consistently. We can use being consistent to improve the quality of our lives or to remain the same. The choice is ours. Any tool can be used to hurt or to heal. Our motives and how we use the tool make all the difference.

Day 245

Integrity

I used to think I was either in integrity or out of it. The issue was very black and white. I am in integrity with myself when I am in alignment with my principles. That hasn't changed for me, but what I have realized is that my principles grow and change as I do. What was honest and loving for me last year may not be what I feel is honest and loving today. I can't demand that anyone else agree or adhere to my definition of integrity; it is, after all, my definition.

How do you define *integrity*? How do you disconnect from yourself and step out of integrity? Find one thing that causes you to step out of your personal definition of integrity, and today make a different choice.

Day 246

Being Intimate

I think of intimacy as "into-me-see." When I'm intimate with myself, I'm aware of my true wants and needs. When I'm really taking care of myself, I can truly be intimate with others.

It is only by being intimate with others and ourselves that we can hope to connect with the divine. We can't become one with the creator alone. Deep intimacy requires vulnerability. It can be frightening to let someone see your light and dark sides, to let someone see you as you are.

Today share some of your fears about intimacy with someone close to you—make sure you share your fears not your thoughts.

Day 247

Dolphin Magic: A Meditation

You find yourself swimming in the midst of a pod of dolphins. They swim below you and around you. You can feel their love. You can hear them singing in the water. A mother dolphin with her young swims beside you. You look into the mother's eye and get lost in her gaze. You swim along with her for some time.

You look down and watch the dolphins perform their graceful ballet. The water is full of their love. You can feel it in every cell of your body. You smile and let the magic and wonder of the dolphins fill your heart and your mind.

DAY 248

Playing with the Energy

Imagine collecting a ball of energy with your hands. Keep adding energy to the ball until it is huge, then throw it into the air and release it.

Collect another ball of energy and fill it with love, peace, and joy. Then place it on your head and allow your body to absorb it.

Collect a third ball of energy. Fill it with images of your dreams, and throw it into the air. Imagine it going to the heart of the universe.

Day 249

Playing with Your Brain

Focus your attention on the right side of your brain. Close your eyes, take a few deep breaths, and put all of your attention on the right side of your head. Now focus your attention on the left side of your brain.

Slowly begin to focus on first the right side and then the left side. Continue going back and forth until you can easily change the focus of your attention. Imagine your attention swinging back and forth like a clock's pendulum.

Once you have mastered this, add another component. Start by focusing your attention on the left side of your brain, move to the right side, and then swing down to your heart. Practice until you can easily shift your attention into your heart.

Day 250

Gazing

Gaze at an object, letting your focus soften; don't look directly at the object. Practice gazing at objects like this and eventually you will begin to see their energy rather than the objects. When I gaze at an object, I am fully present in the center of my being. When I look at an object, I am often not connected with myself. Gazing and looking feel very different from each other.

Practice the art of gazing without really looking at life.

Day 251

Sacred Spaces

Create a sacred space for yourself. Perhaps you'll want to use your altar (see page 234). You can light candles or place fresh flowers there, burn incense, or do anything else to make the space feel sacred to you. Or choose a place outdoors that feels sacred. Create a place to connect with your divinity and visit it often.

Our minds are creatures of habit. If every time you stand in your sacred space you focus on connecting with your divinity, eventually you will feel the connection the moment you stand there.

DAY 252

Eyes of Love

Imagine putting on a pair of magical glasses. When you look through them, all you can see is love. Wear them for the day. When the Grandmother saw the injured wolf she said, "I knew I should fear him, but deep in my being a question arose: 'What would love do?' . . . The earth is sacred; we must love it and treat everything in it with love." Look at your world through the eyes of love.

chapter 10

Circle of Light

The women walked hand-in-hand toward the great circle of rocks watching the young girls walk nervously before them. The air was full of magic. The young girls had spent months preparing for this ceremony. They had carefully beaded their dresses and decorated their baskets, which they carried with great pride.

In the middle of the circle stood the Grandmother dressed in her white ceremonial gown. Her face shone with love. As she guided each woman to her place in the circle, she took a rattle from the altar, said a silent prayer, and handed it to the woman. The young girls stood outside the circle, waiting. When the last woman was seated, the Grandmother stood and raised her arms and began to chant. After a few minutes she said a prayer.

"Great Mother, we give thanks for your wisdom, power, and strength. We ask for your guidance and protection. We ask that our hearts and our minds be open to receive the gifts so freely given. May your divinity awaken within each of us, and may we freely share the blessings we receive this night."

With that the Grandmother nodded her head, and the young girls walked into the center of the circle. The air began to shimmer as they approached the rock altar. They each placed a basket lovingly on the huge rock and stepped back, head bowed, eyes wide with wonder.

The Grandmother stood and moved her hands silently over each girl's basket. She blessed each one and looked at the girls. The bulk of their lives was before them. One of these girls would some day take over her duties, but which one would it be? The Grandmother knew the time had come for her to begin to train her successor.

She sat back on her heels and rocked as she prayed and chanted. She went deep into the dreamtime and stood before the ancestors. The women stood, raised their rattles over their heads, and began to sing and dance. The rhythm took the Grandmother deeper and deeper. She surrendered totally, and the ancestors began to speak.

"We are well pleased with you, my child. You have walked in love and taught many. You will continue to live and love and laugh for many moons.

"The journey home is one of love. You have learned to love well. When you look at the young woman who will take your place, you will see yourself and remember some of the hardship of your early years. You need not protect her. Elders often want to help others with the wisdom they have gained. They want to help others avoid the mistakes they made. But remember, my child, there are no mistakes.

"Every event in your life is a gift, especially the times you think of as the hard times. But if you remember to step into your center and connect with that inner wisdom, all of life becomes easier and filled with lightness and joy. Struggle and pain are always an indication that you have stepped into separation again.

"When you stand in that circle of light, we all stand together, side by side in dominion. When you see yourself in the center of a circle of light, you step into the energy of creation and unleash the magic and wonder of the universe. You are loved, you are love, and you are the gift. Go and remind others that they live in dominion and that the gifts of that circle are always available; they just need to ask."

The Grandmother slowly opened her eyes. The moonlight bathed the circle of women. They always gathered in a circle of light, but tonight that image took on new meaning. She motioned for the young women to come forward and take their baskets. She hugged them each as they proudly received their symbol of womanhood. She held her successor especially close and asked her to come and visit in the morning.

Day 253

Snowflakes

As a young girl I remember catching snowflakes on my mitten, looking at their complex patterns, and watching them as they slowly melted. Some snowflakes were huge, while others were so tiny they looked like small balls of frozen water. When you sit inside at night, all cozy and warm with the outside light turned on, snowflakes look so peaceful as they drift by the window. On a very cold night, when the moon is shining, a field of snow glistens, resembling millions of tiny diamonds. As you walk on the crusty snow, your footsteps crunch, and the sound of your breathing echoes on the frigid air.

A single snowflake is quite harmless, but many snowflakes together create a powerful force. An avalanche can erase a whole village and bury unsuspecting skiers in an instant.

See your life as many snowflakes—single thoughts or actions, beliefs, agreements, assumptions, habits, and routines. Each taken separately is of little significance, but when you put them all together you have the major events in your life, the avalanches.

Take time today to examine your thoughts. Ask yourself throughout the day: "What am I thinking?" Then drop down a little and notice what emotions are present. Scan your body and notice your physical sensations. Once you have gone beyond your filter system, ask yourself what you need to do right now. What small adjustment do you need to make to avoid an avalanche in the future? What do you need to do for yourself that would feel loving and nurturing and really add to the quality of your life?

DAY 254

The Truth

What is the truth? The truth is relative. From the limited perspective of our minds, we can't possibly hope to know the truth about anything. Yet, we get so attached to the truth. Often we choose to be right rather than to be happy.

Notice how you feel about the truth. How do you feel when you consider the idea that there is no such thing as the truth? Explore the idea of truth and see how often you are willing to defend what you believe to be the truth.

DAY 255

Perfection

You are absolutely perfect just the way you are. There is no need to change anything.

When you know you already are perfect, you can begin to move toward pleasure in your life instead of moving away from pain. You can change something simply because you want to change, not because you feel you "need" to.

Look in the mirror, look directly into your eyes, and tell yourself, "I am perfect just the way I am." Keep reminding yourself of that until you believe it.

Day 256

Gentleness

I often remind people to be gentle and loving as they explore their filter system. Gentleness is one of the most powerful tools we can use to heal our emotional wounds or to release our limitations.

What is your reaction to the concept of gentleness? Do you consider it a sign of weakness or strength? Is being gentle beneficial or something to avoid? How could you apply the concept of gentleness in your life?

Day 257

Commitment

The idea of committing to anything is scary for some people. How strong is your commitment to yourself, to your happiness, and to achieving your personal freedom? I struggled for a long time with the idea of putting my needs and myself first.

Do you need to release any beliefs before you can really put yourself first? What does making a commitment to yourself mean to you? How does it feel? What are you really committed to creating in your life? Are you willing to make a commitment to yourself and your happiness?

Day 258

Acceptance

We are adventurers constantly exploring the nature of reality in hope of finding out who we really are.

Acceptance is the cornerstone of a happy life. Life is as it is—if we deny what is, we create a great deal of unhappiness, stress, and discomfort in our lives. We also limit our range of emotions, our options, and our ability to make choices.

Acceptance comes from a Latin word meaning "to take to oneself that which is offered." Part of acceptance is realizing that everything in life is a gift, especially the experiences that we say we don't like. Good or bad, every experience is an opportunity to connect with our divinity and our true nature or to move farther into fear and denial. In fact, we are explorers; we are constantly exploring the nature of reality as well as our true nature.

The first step toward happiness is to accept where we are and decide if that is where we want to stay. If we fail to accept where we are, change becomes more difficult.

Try closing your eyes, spinning around several times, and then walking out of the room without opening your eyes. It is possible but awkward. Now pretend you are in a different building and do the same exercise. It becomes even more difficult to navigate. Life becomes much easier to negotiate when we open our eyes, see our filter system, and make decisions based on what we'd like to experience. Acceptance allows us to focus on what *is* rather than on what we *think* is.

Day 259

Big Bubble: A Meditation

You are walking on the beach. Your feet barely leave a trace as you stroll along the white sand. You spy hundreds of bits of shells, tiny pieces of coral, and wonderful pebbles of all different colors resting on the sand. A gentle, warm breeze blows the clouds, big and fluffy, across the sky, which is the most amazing shade of blue. You feel at peace, relaxed, and at ease.

A large bubble begins to move toward you and you approach it. The surface of the bubble is iridescent, and it shimmers in the sunlight. When you look into the bubble you see yourself as you are, rather than how you think you are. You see yourself as a radiant being of light surrounded by hundreds of other beings of light. The wind stirs, blowing the bubble into the surf. You notice countless other bubbles floating on the waves, becoming one with the waves. You smile and walk on.

day 260

Doing the Work

If you want to achieve personal freedom, there is no doubt you have to take action. I often refer to that as doing the work. What emotions do you have attached to doing the work? Do you think of it as hard and painful, or do you think of it as fun, exciting, and joyful?

Today notice what you tell yourself about this journey. If you think it is hard, it certainly will be. "Every event in your life is a gift, especially the times you think of as the hard times," said the ancesters to the Grandmother. "But if you remember to step into your center and connect with that inner wisdom, all of life becomes easier and filled with lightness and joy."

Day 261

Journaling

I spent weeks looking for just the right pen and journal before I seriously started journaling. In hindsight I see that it was as good an excuse as any to avoid writing. Don't procrastinate. Today spend thirty minutes writing. Put down whatever comes to mind. Sit and write no matter how you feel about doing it. After practicing in this manner for a few days or a couple weeks, you will find you no longer want to avoid writing.

day 262

Having Fun

How do you define *fun*? What if your definition included things like emotional clearing, recapitulation, tracking, meditating, and writing? What if you felt going to work was having fun? How would your life change if you defined everything as fun? Have fun redefining having fun.

Day 263

Try

Trying is an activity that we can use to limit our experience and our progress. If we say we will try to do something, we seldom actually do it. Trying in no way indicates doing, it is merely the attempt. Trying implies not accomplishing. We either choose to do something or we don't. Trying doesn't even fit into the equation.

We can try something new by taking action or we can use trying as an excuse not to actually do the thing at all. Keep track today of how often you use the word *try* and how you use it.

Day 264

Letting Go

Hold a pen in the palm of your hand. Turn your palm face up and open your hand. You have let go of the pen but you are still holding onto it. Now turn your hand over and let the pen fall to the floor. Feel the difference. How often do you let go of things in your life with your palm facing upward?

DAY 265

Making Decisions

The next time you have a hard time making a decision flip a coin. If it comes up heads and you are glad, you have your decision. If it comes up tails and you want to try two out of three tosses, you still have your decision. If the answer isn't a wholehearted yes, then the answer is really no.

Can you ever really make a wrong choice? If you go left often enough, you'll wind up where you would have had you taken a right.

Allow yourself to have fun making decisions. When in doubt today, flip a coin.

Day 266

Having and Wanting: A Meditation

Think of something you want—something you have wanted for a very long time. Remember how it feels to really want something. Notice how your body feels. Breathe deeply and connect with the feeling of wanting.

Think of something you have had for a very long time—something you know you will have for a long time to come. Feel the sense of peace and acceptance that having brings. Breathe deeply and connect with that knowing, that sense of having. Notice how wanting and having feel different.

Think back to a time before you had an object, when you wanted it but didn't yet have it. Remember how you shifted from a place of wanting to one of having. Take a few deep breaths and practice shifting from wanting to having.

DAY 267

Being Right or Wrong

The ideas of right or wrong limit our experience of life. How often do you feel
the need to judge someone or something as right or wrong? How do you
feel about letting go of the concepts of right and wrong? "Remember, my
child," the ancestors told the Grandmother, "there are no mistakes."

day 268

Attachments

A hot air balloon can't rise if it's tethered to the ground. Neither can you be free as long as you have attachments.

Our thoughts alone won't create our limitations; it is our attachments to our thoughts that do. Make a list of all the things you have attachments to. Sever these lines of attachment and watch your balloon rise with ease.

Day 269

Energy Lines

When I look at life as an energy system, I see energy lines intersecting and interweaving. Everything is interconnected. If you exert energy in one place, it affects the whole system.

When you go out walking you can connect with the energy lines and use them to augment your energy. The energy lines can assist you as you climb, help you be more sensitive to the energies around you, and remind you to be more mindful.

As you walk, focus your attention on your hands and feel the energy as you move your hands back and forth.

DAY 270

Looking Good

When we were learning how to walk, we fell down a lot more than we stood up. If we had been worried about looking good when we learned to walk, we'd probably still be crawling on all fours.

One of my mentors told me early in my process that you can't look good while you're exploring your filter system. As a result of this wisdom, I gave myself permission to make mistakes and even look foolish if necessary. I would do whatever I needed in order to achieve personal freedom.

What does it feel like to want to look good? Notice whether wanting to look good affects your process in any way.

DAY 271

Mother Earth: A Meditation

With the eyes of love Mother Earth sees the beauty and wonder of the planet as only she can. She looks at all of her children with compassion and joy.

Imagine yourself standing in the presence of Mother Earth. She is a gentle soul with an open heart and a forgiving nature. She tenderly embraces you as she does all her children. Her love and compassion touch the very core of your being. You connect with her spirit at a profound level. You know she will always be there for you and that all your needs will be met.

You see her essence in the sky, the trees, the animals, the clothes you wear, and the food you eat. You can begin to see her spirit in everything, including the highways and the cities. You feel her presence in your body as you breathe and move about your day. You realize that no matter where you are, she is also there. You see the great Earth Mother everywhere and realize that together you are the caretakers of this world.

Day 272

Shadows and Candles

Put a candle in the center of a darkened room. Sit facing a wall with the candle behind you. Watch your shadow. Breathe deeply and be in the presence of your shadow. Play with it, experience the energy of your shadow, and observe your mind.

Move the candle around until your shadow fills the room. Allow for the possibility that your shadow creates you rather than you creating it. Ask your shadow what it would like to tell you and then listen. See what you can learn from your shadow.

Day 273

Chanting

Chanting helps to quiet the mind's endless chatter by providing a neutral focus. The simplest chant is the word OM (pronounced with a long o). Take a deep breath and as you slowly exhale say the word OM. Chant a round o until you are almost out of air and then slide into the m sound. Allow your whole body to resonate with the sound. Play with the sounds until they feel right to you.

Find some old chants and memorize one. Let the sounds of the chant fill your heart, mind, and body.

DAY 274

The Senses

Read through this exercise, then close your eyes, and slowly repeat it three times.

Take a few deep breaths and focus your attention on your hearing. Notice all the sounds you can hear. Really pay attention. Next focus your attention on your sense of smell. Breathe deeply, sample the air, and really smell. Now focus your attention on your sense of taste—breathe through your mouth and taste the air. Shift your attention to your sense of touch. What do you feel? Notice your clothes, where your body touches anything, the temperature of the air; notice what you can feel on your body, with your body, and within your body. Just barely open your eyes and look around. Take in all the details, the colors, the textures, and the shapes. What can you see?

As you go about your day, spend a little time paying attention to your five senses. Practice feeling the world around you and notice how it affects you.

DAY 275

The Temple: A Meditation

As you descend into the valley, you see the sun glistening off the roof of the temple. Your heart pounds joyously as you enter the outer gardens. The marble stairs are rounded and worn yet spotless. Urns of fragrant herbs sit on either side of the entrance.

As you approach, two priestesses walk silently out of the temple, descend the stairs, and embrace you. They've been waiting for you for a very long time. They lead you up the stairs and into the temple. You walk directly up to the altar and kneel down on a velvet pillow.

The coolness of the temple soothes you. The temple's power and gentleness touches the core of your being and fills you with its wisdom and strength. You bow your head and give thanks. So many questions well up within you, but you know they will all be answered. You are home at last.

Day 276

Nothing You Need

You could choose to change your thinking and your life would be very different if you released some of your limiting thought patterns. But you don't need to do that unless you want to change your life. There is nothing you need to learn, nothing you need to overcome, and nothing you need to change.

When you find yourself needing something, make a choice instead. For instance, you don't need to stop being judgmental; instead, you can choose to think more lovingly. If you want to be more spiritual, be so. If you want peace of mind, think so. And if you want change, become so.

DAY 277

Gratitude

Gratitude is a very powerful energy. When we are truly grateful, fear no longer exists. Practice feeling gratitude today and see what happens.

If you find yourself stuck in traffic, be grateful you have a car to drive. If you have a lot of bills to pay, be grateful you have an income. If you have a lot of work to do, be grateful you have a job. Whenever you resist or don't feel like doing a task, find a way to be grateful for having the ability to do it.

Day 278

Your Favorite Song

Listen to the words of your favorite song. What do the lyrics say about you? What do they tell you about your filter system? What exactly makes it your favorite song? Is it a specific lyric? Does it generate a certain emotion?

Day 279

Dreams

Dreams can act as powerful messengers. To harness the power of your dreams, begin keeping a dream journal. Put a notebook on your nightstand or in the bathroom and make short notes about your dreams every morning. Tell yourself just before you go to sleep that you can easily remember your dreams. During the day, remind yourself occasionally that you will easily remember your dreams even if that hasn't been the truth in the past. If you do have a hard time, drink several glasses of water before you go to bed. When you get up to use the bathroom, write down the dreams you were having until that point!

Day 280

The Gift

Every day we send ourselves gifts that, if carefully unwrapped, will set us free. Each event in our lives is a wonderful opportunity to uncover the real cause of our limitations. We can change our minds and release ourselves from our limitations at any time. Unfortunately we get so engrossed in the wrappings, the event, and our thoughts that we forget to unwrap the present, our freedom.

Find the gift in every moment today. Whenever you find yourself having an emotional reaction, remember that the cause of the reaction is not the event or someone else's behavior, but your own thoughts.

chapter 11

The Love and the Laughter

Long ago the ancient ones stood together as the mists of creation swirled about them and they asked, "Who am I? What am I?" The mists parted and millions of universes emerged. The ancient ones looked upon their creation with love. There were stars and planets, light and dark, and galaxies everywhere. The wind of creation raced through the universe whispering and asking, "Who am I?" The ancient ones were delighted with their creation; joy filled their hearts, and laughter filled the air.

But there was no one to hear so they decided to create a special world in each galaxy, a place that was sacred and unique. They filled some planets with magnificent crystal structures, some were divided into land and water, while others were swirling masses of vapors that continued to recreate themselves.

The universe was beautiful, but it was also very empty. There were no beings to enjoy its magnificence. One planet was very special to the ancient ones so they filled it with plants and flowers that had wonderful smells and vibrant colors. They created magical things like babbling brooks, mountains, rainbows, and waterfalls. They set the wind free upon this planet. It softly caressed the world and whispered the secrets of the universe, but there was still no one to hear.

Next they created animals of all shapes and sizes. They filled the ocean with fish and whales and dolphins. The ancient ones looked upon their creation and they were pleased, but there was still something missing. The ancient ones again asked the question and found no answer. So they decided to try an experiment—they created beings in their own likeness. They placed a piece of themselves inside each one. They gave the beings the power to create and the freedom of choice and hoped they would use these gifts wisely. They placed this power deep within the beings' spirits.

Because the ancient ones created the world in love, it reflected their harmony and grace. All the systems were perfectly balanced. The needs of all the creatures were easily met and the world was a safe and loving place. All the creatures felt the love that surrounded them and knew they were safe. They had no fear.

The ancient ones gave human beings the ability to see the truth in all things, but the choice to do so was theirs and theirs alone. The ancient ones would never intrude upon a person's free will, but they remained always available to help.

As time went on humans moved farther and farther away from their connection with their creators. Their spirits grew restless as they forgot their true nature. Eventually humans began to know fear. Fear became their god, but love continued to wait, it was always there just a breath away. The farther people moved away from their connection to love, the more painful their existence became.

Eventually, when the pain became intense enough, the people began to ask, "Who am I? Why am I here?" At that moment the ancient ones reached out and the journey toward love began.

Day 281

Agreements

Our filter system is composed of our beliefs, assumptions, agreements, and our attachments. Those filters effectively stop us from experiencing intimacy with others, our divinity, and ourselves. As long as we see our filter system instead of "reality," we can't and won't remember ourselves or experience our divine nature.

We all have agreements with ourselves, society, the people close to us, and God. Look at your life honestly—everything is in your life because you have made an agreement to have it there; what isn't in your life isn't there because at some level you have an agreement to keep it out.

Let's start with a simple agreement, such as the speed limit. Most of get from one place to another using some form of transportation—many of us drive cars. When we get a license, we supposedly agree to obey the speed limit—but do we?

Here in Hawaii, the state used traffic vans to monitor speeders and mailed tickets to speeding drivers. The public outcry was fierce, and even though the vans curtailed speeding, they were removed.

My car received a speeding ticket while I was out of the country. I got angry at first, but then I reminded myself that there is no "out there." I wasn't upset by the ticket; I was upset by what I had been telling myself. I could have simply focused on the fact that I was out of the country and that a friend of mine was driving the car, but I chose to go deeper. When I noticed my reaction, I realized I hadn't really agreed to obey some of society's traffic laws. I used the ticket as an opportunity to notice what it felt like when an agreement was enforced—or in this case what the enforcement of my lack of agreement felt like.

Much of our life is controlled by our agreements. Observe what yours are. Do you say yes when you want to say no? Do you cut into lines? Do you speed? Do you cheat on your taxes? Are you habitually on time or late? Do you judge others for judging you? Do you expect yourself to be perfect?

Day 282

Limitations

What do you consider a limitation? How do you define limitations? How do they affect your life?

Every limitation you experience originates in your filter system. There are no limitations. Your mind might argue that you can't walk on fire, but I have led many fire walks and people seldom burn their feet.

The more violently my mind resists looking at a belief, the greater freedom I experience once I release it. Our filter system stops us from being able to see our limitations, but we can see the result of those limiting beliefs in our lives. Every event, every limitation we experience, is really a gateway either to freedom or to our self-imposed prison.

You are a limitless being and your spirit chafes against your limitations constantly. It pushes you toward your true nature. Your limitations will set you free. And you are free to choose how and when.

Make a list of your limitations. How can you view them as assets rather than liabilities?

Day 283

Mind Chatter

Your mind constantly talks to you. It's likely that you are often unconscious of this mind chatter, yet you make your decisions based upon it.

Today, notice the noise your mind makes. Pause several times as you move throughout your day and notice your thoughts. If they are harsh or judgmental, take some time to say something gentle, loving, and accepting instead. See if changing your thoughts changes how you approach things.

Day 284

Hard

A lot of people tell me what a hard time they have doing the exercises. They talk about how this process is hard work. If you believe life is hard, it will be. If you believe life is fun, it will be. Do you want to continue to believe that life is hard?

How often do you use the word *hard*? Take a deep breath and think of something you consider hard. How does that feel? Now take another deep breath and imagine the same thing as easy. How does easy feel? Today whenever you consider something hard, take a deep breath, and feel it as easy instead. Make a list of all the things you think are hard and spend some time focusing on each one becoming easy. See what practicing easy instead of hard does to your daily life.

Day 285

Accepting What Is: A Meditation

What is simply is. Breathe in that thought. There is no right or wrong; there is only what is. Feel your fear and resistance to what is rise to the surface of your consciousness. Fight if you must, resist, scream, yell, and wish it wasn't so.

Feel the futility of the battle. What is still is as it is. Feel yourself resisting it, judging it, trying to change it with every fiber of your being. Imagine yourself having a cosmic tug of war with what is. How tiring.

Remember the tug of war exercise? Drop your end of the rope. Hold hands with what is and imagine both of you dancing around a circle. As you move your perspective changes. You see things differently. Everything changes, yet nothing has changed.

Step into a place within yourself where you can accept what is for what it is. You don't have to like it, you simply have to accept it. Breathe in the energy of acceptance and observe your perspective of what is.

Day 286

The Journey to Find the Real You

True freedom comes when you have a deep, real, and abiding connection with your spirit. Developing that connection is a journey that can happen in a moment or take a lifetime. How long it takes matters little; what does matter is that you take all the time you need. Daily practice will serve you well.

As you journey within, you will find three main levels of consciousness. The first thing you become aware of is your thoughts. After you go a little deeper, you become aware of your emotions. Below that are your feelings or physical sensations.

Take a moment several times during the day to go inside. Notice your thoughts, travel into and through your emotions, and then notice what you are feeling deep within your body. It is through these feelings that you connect with your spirit.

Our thoughts and emotions generate feelings in our bodies, but so does the energy that surrounds us. It will take time and practice to discern the difference. Don't worry about not being able to do this or about having to do it perfectly. Just experiment, play, and engage your innate curiosity.

Train yourself to feel the energy all around you without naming it. Just feel and be with the feelings.

day 287

What Do You Need?

Take a deep breath and notice your thoughts. Go beyond your thoughts and notice your emotions. Now go deeper and notice what you are feeling in your body.

Ask yourself, "What do I want? What do I need?" Sit in the silence and let the answers come. Do this often as you move through your day.

Day 288

Knowing

Most of my life I pursued knowledge. I discovered that knowledge and wisdom are very different, and of the two, wisdom will serve you far better. Societies based on domination encourage us to believe that knowledge is power. When I began my spiritual explorations, people talked to me about developing a sense of inner knowing. I spent years getting in touch with that knowing only to realize that knowing was often the biggest obstacle to connecting to my divinity.

Once I know something, I cut myself off from my essence, from God, and from true happiness. Within each of us there is the quiet, still voice of the spirit. Often the mind's desire to feel safe will masquerade as that voice. We will "know" only to find out later it was the mind at work not the spirit after all.

It takes years of practice to develop discernment. If you feel confusion, fear, or resistance, chances are they emanate from your mind. Explore what the concept of inner wisdom means to you. How is it different from knowledge? Is your desire to have that inner knowing related to your need to feel safe? Can you know something and, in the moment, be open to any possibility? Does knowing really serve you?

day 289

Intimacy

Are you willing to allow people to see who and what you really are? Are you willing to let people see even the darkest parts of your being? Does your desire to be liked stop you from being able to say no to others?

In order to be intimate with another, we must first learn how to be intimate with ourselves. Intimacy ("into-me-see") is much easier when we love ourselves so much that what others think doesn't matter. When we love ourselves, it is much easier to be open and let intimacy into our lives. Practice opening your heart, remind yourself you are safe, and fill yourself up with the love that always surrounds you. Don't let fear become your god; as the ancient ones knew, love is only a breath away.

Day 290

Sacredness

Imagine living your life as if each moment were sacred. Imagine that everything you look at, everything you touch, and everything that touches you is sacred. Imagine the act of living as a sacred act itself.

Take a deep breath and call upon the energy of sacredness; let it fill your heart and your mind. Feel the sacredness within you and around you. How does it feel to you? What would happen to your life if you made every moment sacred? If taking a shower became a sacred act for you, how would the water feel? Or if preparing a meal became a sacred act, how much better would the food taste? Practice making even the most mundane actions in your life sacred and see what happens.

DAY 291

Silence

Observing silence is a powerful practice. Even if you simply decide to hold silence for just an hour or two, the power will amaze you. The first time I did this I realized how much energy I expend with my words. Set aside at least one day a month to be in silence. No music, no TV, no reading—just silence.

Make silence a sacred game. Notice how so often we avoid silence or, in the midst of chaos, crave it. Play with silence. Notice your reaction to being still, notice how restless your mind can be, notice the noises with which we fill our world.

DAY 292

Your Shadow Self: A Meditation

You feel very peaceful and at ease as you walk along the beautiful path. Occasionally the trees part and you see the valley below and the ocean glistening in the distance. You've walked this path before, but never has it looked so serene and lovely.

The altar in the clearing is more beautiful than you remember it. You approach slowly and deliberately. On the other side of the altar you see your shadow self. It looks frail and tiny one moment, then appears huge and threatening.

You take another look at your shadow self, walk up to the altar, place your hands on its surface, and bow your head in prayer. Your heart is full of love and acceptance. You walk around the altar and greet your shadow self. As you look into its eyes, your heart fills with compassion. The fear and loneliness you see there touches you deeply.

Pick up your shadow self and lovingly place it on the altar. Place your hands on its heart and begin the ceremony. Love surrounds you both, and you feel the old pain lifting. You see your shadow self as a part of you, and you understand the gifts it brings to your life.

Release your fear, anger, and resentment, and see how your separation from others caused the pain. Allow yourself to become one. You know there will always be a dark side to your nature. You choose love and you choose to love even the darkest parts of yourself. In that acceptance you find compassion—for yourself, for everyone you know, for everyone you'll ever meet, for everyone who fills your being. You find freedom and joy as you embrace the totality of life.

Day 293

Change Is a Breath Away

Pause during the day and take a few long, slow, deep breaths. Allow your breathing to take you into the very core of your being. If you find yourself getting impatient with someone you care about, take a deep breath and ask yourself what loving thing you could do. We either choose how to act or how to react to life.

Whenever you find yourself reacting, take a few deep breaths, get back into your center, and ask yourself, "What would love do?"

DAY 294

Playing with Clothes

We each have a style or a way of dressing we find most comfortable. Be different from your usual way of dressing today. If you dress conservatively, be outrageous. If you are often trendy, dress very conservatively.

Wear two different shoes. Put your clothes on inside out. Simply wear a hat. Or dye your hair pink. Be wild and crazy. Play with how you dress.

DAY 295

Strength

What are your greatest strengths? What does it take to be strong? Do you need a great deal of strength to stay on your path or to change your life? Are strength and ease alike or dissimilar? What role does strength play in your life?

Day 296

Shadows

Go outside early in the morning or late in the afternoon when your shadow is the longest. Find a place where you won't be disturbed and look at your shadow. Breathe deeply and watch your shadow; move, interact with it, and focus on feeling your shadow.

Play with the idea that your shadow is real and you are its reflection. Spend time with your shadow. It can assist you in experiencing other energy states.

DAY 297

Dying

In the Toltec tradition, death is thought to be our greatest teacher as well as our most formidable opponent. Embracing death removes our fear of it and can enhance our ability to remember our true nature.

Life is a terminal illness. From the moment we are born, we begin to die. If today were your last day on earth, what would you do? Make a list of all the things you'd want to do if you knew you only had a year to live. Start doing them.

Day 298

Reviewing Your Day

Before you go to sleep each night, review your day from the moment you got up until the moment you got in bed. If there is any energy attached to any part of the day, release it. If you have some unfinished business, make a note to finish it tomorrow. Before you go to sleep, make sure you have finished your day.

We tend to spend a good part of our dreams clearing out the day. If you go to sleep with a clean slate, you will have time to explore and have fun in your dreams.

DAY 299

Belonging: A Meditation

Imagine yourself standing in a dimly lit room feeling disconnected and lonely. Take a few deep breaths and feel that sense of isolation. Just be with it: breathe it in, accept it, and embrace it.

The lights in the room become brighter and brighter. As you look around, realize the room is filled with other people who feel as you do. Someone starts to laugh, and one by one, everyone joins in. Each of you realizes you have always belonged. People who want to support you have surrounded you all of your life. It was your fear that stopped you from being able to see them.

Allow yourself to be filled with that sense of belonging.

DAY 300

Walking

Set aside five minutes and pay attention to every step you take. Walk slowly and mindfully. Be fully conscious of each foot as it rises and falls. Notice your weight as it shifts from leg to leg. Move quickly and then move in slow motion.

With every step, you leave behind an energy imprint. Are you leaving love or fear in your wake?

DAY 301

Floating

Floating is so freeing. We can all float, even if our fear stops us from doing so easily. Find some place you can float. Surrender yourself to the water and let the water support you. Feel how effortlessly the water can support your body. Now allow for the possibility that the universe can support all of your hopes and dreams just as easily as the water supports your body.

DAY 302

Power Spots

In any given area there is a spot where you will gain energy, one where you will leak energy, and one where you will experience a sense of confusion. Pick a room in your house and slowly move around it. Sit in different spots. Close your eyes, take a few deep breaths, and notice how each spot feels.

Notice whether you are attracted to a spot where you gain energy, leak energy, or feel confused. Depending on your filter system you will have your favorite spots.

DAY 303

The Face of God: A Meditation

You find yourself flying through space, going faster and faster. You fly past hundreds of galaxies. The stars race by, and you feel incredibly free. The darkness of space embraces you.

As you approach the center of the universe, your heart opens. You feel a loving presence, a presence so vast and encompassing you aren't sure where you begin and it ends. The love is almost overwhelming. You feel so safe and at peace.

You start to slow down. The light has become so bright you can hardly see. It bathes you in its warmth. You move closer to the center, to the light, and the feeling of love builds ever larger. Find yourself standing in the presence of God. You look up at the face of God and are amazed by its beauty, its love, its total acceptance. You know without a doubt that you are loved and accepted just the way you are.

DAY 304

Programming Your Dreams

Once you remember your dreams on a regular basis, you can start to use them in a variety of fun and enlightening ways.

Ask for a dream to clarify something. Just before you go to sleep think about what you would like to access in your dreams. Write your question down and then record your dreams the next morning. With a little practice you can access any information you want in your dreams, even solutions to waking dilemmas in your life. If you don't understand a dream, ask for another dream to clarify it.

You can also ask for healing in your dreams. Or you can visit people and places. Sweet dreams.

DAY 305

Grace

I have had many unexpected gifts as I have walked my path. Meeting Sister Sarita and don Miguel Ruiz was a gift, totally unexpected and not sought after. There have been times I could have died, yet here I am happily alive and grateful for every moment of my existence. I think of grace as an unexpected gift. Grace, to me, is an unmerited intervention by the divine—those magical coincidences in life, chance meetings, and strong internal hunches.

What does *grace* mean to you? Have you ever experienced the gift of grace in your life? Do you have an emotional response to the idea of grace? I used to. I was afraid if grace brought something into my life that it could just as easily be taken away from me. Today my safe universe is full of gratitude and grace. Play with the idea of grace and see where it takes you.

Day 306

Candles

I love candles. They're wonderful tools for meditation. They can make a special place sacred with their gentle flames, warmth, and earthy smell. I have an altar in my office, and every time I open my office I mindfully light the candles on the altar, say a prayer, and set my intent for the day. When I want to focus my attention on an issue in my life, I often light a small tea candle, say a prayer, and let the candle burn until it extinguishes itself.

When you extinguish a candle, do so mindfully, with gratitude and with a prayer of thanks for its love, light, and healing. Light a candle and feel its energy fill the room.

Day 307

You Are a Magician

You are a magician. You take your thoughts, make decisions, and create your experiences of life. Your ability to make choices is your magic wand. What will you use it to create?

Today consciously create an experience. Decide to feel something and then create the feeling.

Day 308

The Sum of the Parts

Your essence is divided into many parts: your spirit, your small self, your big self, the little child, the rebellious teenager, the part of you that feels superior to everyone else, the part that feels inferior, the angry part, the sad part—the list goes on and on. As you move toward integration you become larger than before you fragmented. Perhaps that is what this process is all about.

Imagine you and all your parts sitting around a huge round table having a celebration. What would all those parts have to say to you and one another?

chapter 12

Life Is But a Dream

All his life he had been a seeker. He traveled the world looking for the truth, always searching, yet he never found that sense of peace and knowing he so desperately wanted. He had dedicated himself to finding the meaning of life, to finding God, but he'd failed.

With each passing year it became harder to continue. He valiantly fought against the quiet voice within him that suggested he surrender. He vowed he would never give up.

But he knew he was dying. He had failed. An immense feeling of sadness overwhelmed him, and he no longer had the energy to fight. The only thing he could do was surrender.

Suddenly one of the ancient ones stood before him. The man rubbed his eyes in amazement and in a frail voice, asked, "Why now? Where have you been all of my life?"

The ancient one answered, "I have always been here, but you've been too busy searching to see me. You fought so hard that you couldn't hear the voice of love above the chatter of your mind. You howled so loudly you could only hear yourself. You cannot fill a cup that is already full."

"What do you mean?" asked the man. "My only prayer has been for enlightenment. How dare you say I have been too busy to listen? I have spent all my time searching!"

"Exactly," said the ancient one. "You searched but you didn't allow yourself to find what you sought. You were afraid of love. You listened only to your fear, you fought your heart, and you were too afraid to accept love. You ignored the whispers of your spirit. You let fear become your God. You searched for peace but you never allowed yourself to be at peace."

"What is there to find in anyone's heart but sentimental drivel?" the man retorted. "If one works very hard and learns to control his emotions, perhaps he will be fortunate enough to find enlightenment. If one suffers long enough and learns to master himself then, and only then, will he be the master of his fate."

The ancient one smiled sadly and said, "Do you truly believe you can find enlightenment by controlling things? What of compassion? What of love? Love demands nothing."

"Love is fine for the masses but the truly enlightened have no need for emotions.

Emotions are a sign of weakness. Compassion is for people who feel they must prove themselves. I have no need for other people's goodwill."

"Let me tell you a story," said the ancient one. "At the beginning of time, the ancient ones decided to share the gift of immortality with the mortals. They placed the spirit of immortality deep within their beings, knowing it was a place few would have the courage to explore.

"It was decided that at the time of each human's death, an ancient one would come to answer any questions and guide that spirit home. But instead of embracing death, you began to fear it. You believed you were a body instead of enjoying the experience of having one. You forgot you were a spirit who came to live within a body and that you came to earth to have fun and remember your true nature.

"Instead of awakening to your true nature, you continue to go deeper into the dream you call life. None of this is real. All the secrets of the universe lie within you. You cling so tenaciously to a reality 'out there' that doesn't exist. The only thing that is real is your spirit. Your spirit is pure love—expansive, unconditional, limitless love.

"You think of me as the Grim Reaper. I am here to help you find your way home, to remind you of who and what you really are. I cannot force you to listen or to believe me. You are dreaming, my friend. You cannot die. You are already free. You are made of God. You are one with God. You always have been and always will be. That energy you call God is infinite, so how can you not be in the heart of God even now?

"The gift of your spirit or the love that lives within you is precious and freely offered. All you have to do is allow yourself to feel that love. You are living in a beautiful amusement park designed for you and you alone. You are safe, you are loved, and you are immortal.

"Nothing in the universe has the power to hurt you unless you pretend to be hurt. Heaven and hell exist only in your mind. You can create either by how you choose to view life.

"You can see the face of God within everything if only you . . ."

The dying man began to cough violently. When his coughing subsided, he said, "Why do you bother me with this foolishness, old man? Leave me alone so I can die in peace. I don't want to hear your lies anymore." The old man looked around and saw that his visitor had left.

The ancient one smiled. He had sat with this spirit many times before. At least this time they had been able to talk. Maybe in the future this spirit would be more aware of the dream and not get so tightly caught in the web he thought of as reality.

DAY 309

Surrender

When I first moved to Hawaii, I decided to learn how to body board. After a few lessons I went to the beach where the big waves were. Even though the waves looked very rough, I decided to go in. I fought and fought to get beyond the breakers. I was determined.

Suddenly I found myself kneeling in the sand with a huge wave coming toward me. I was afraid, but I valiantly held my board in front of me to protect myself. The wave took me for quite a ride. I thought the last thing I would ever see was white water. After several minutes the wave deposited me on the beach, coughing, sputtering, and very bruised. If I had just surrendered and let the wave wash over me, I would have had a much easier ride.

Life is so much easier when you learn to surrender. What do you resist in your life? What would happen if you surrendered to it?

DAY 310

Ease

Is life hard or easy? Is change hard work? Is change something that brings ease into your life? How much ease do you have in your life? Explore the energy of ease today. How easy is it for you to be at ease?

DAY 311

Wholeness and Holiness

My wholeness allows me to experience my holiness. My search for a connection with my sacred nature demands that I find my wholeness as well. Close your eyes and think about the two words.

Do you ever feel fragmented? Do you feel a profound connection to your holiness? How would your life look if you were wholly present in the moment and your every act felt sacred or holy?

DAY 312

Nothingness

The old seers believed the universe was a hostile place. They believed that at the end of your existence your consciousness was consumed by a force they called the eagle and you ceased to exist. I consider myself a new seer and experience the universe as a safe and loving place. I believe that we eventually step into the nothingness.

The purpose of most spiritual paths is to become one with God. When you become one with the energy of creation, you cease to exist. You become nothing in exchange for becoming everything. The small self no longer exists. The concept of separation makes no sense when we are all one.

My small self fears the nothingness. When I talk about going into the nothingness in my classes there is a great deal of fear and resistance. Explore the idea of nothingness for yourself.

Listen to the sounds around you and focus your attention on the silence between the sounds. Take a deep breath and notice the point where you aren't inhaling or exhaling. Look at the shadows in your world. Focus on where your thoughts begin and end. Find the nothingness in between.

Allow for the possibility that surrendering to the nothingness will take a leap of faith but that what you are really doing is letting go of any sense of separation, which was an illusion in the first place. You become everything in the instant you become nothing.

DAY 313

Freedom: A Meditation

The hard metal clank of the gate shutting sends shivers through your body. You never get used to that sound. You can't remember how long you've been in this prison. The walls seem to get closer with each passing day.

You awaken in the morning like every other day. There is nothing remarkable about it. But when the guard appears at your cell, he says rather gruffly, "Follow me."

He leads you to the gate, it swings wide, and you walk out of the prison of your mind. As you walk away, the guard reminds you, "You've always had the key; you just forgot. You merely had to retrain your mind."

DAY 314

Changing the World

For years I wanted to help change the world. One day as I meditated, the thought came to me, "Who am I to decide the world needs changing? Perhaps the world is perfect just the way it is. Who am I to judge?" I played with that thought for a long time.

I could see plenty of evidence that the world needed fixing; all I had to do was watch the evening news. Then one day I realized the world really was perfect just the way it was. Even though I detested the cruelty, the violence, murder, rape, genocide, and our inhumanity to one another, there was nothing inherently wrong with any of it. I couldn't change the world, but I could change myself. I could become more loving. I could silence my inner violence and cruelty. I could retrain my mind and fill my heart and mind with peace.

On occasion, I still want to change the world, and when I do I go inside and discover what is really upsetting me. I examine my thoughts about what's happening in the world and how those thoughts limit me. Track your thoughts and feelings about wanting to change the world and see where they lead.

DAY 315

Instead of Words

Do we really need words to communicate? My mind responds with a resounding, "Of course we do!" Ninety percent of our communications are nonverbal, yet we still feel we must rely on words.

As long as we depend upon words, we underuse our other means of communication. Today, experiment with nonverbal communications. If someone asks you how to do something, show her rather than tell her. Show people how you feel. Find new ways to communicate. Spend the day communicating without using words.

Day 316

Forgiveness

Forgiveness is a process. The first step is to allow yourself to be as emotional as necessary about an event. Yes, your emotions are self-generated but they are also energy in motion. If you are angry, feel it. Scream, yell, beat the bed, write hate letters you won't send, do whatever you must to release your anger. You certainly don't need to yell *at* someone, but let your anger go. Let the energy of your anger flow out of you. Once you have, forgive yourself and the other person.

We forgive for our own benefit. As we move more fully into dominion we begin to realize there is nothing to forgive, and we can move beyond forgiveness to acceptance of life, events, and people just as they are.

Whom do you need to forgive? Whom do you need to ask forgiveness from? Are you still holding on to anything? Is there anything you still believe is unforgivable? What does the energy of forgiveness feel like? And what does it feel like to hold on to a grudge?

DAY 317

Goals

If goals become an external pursuit, they assist us in stepping back into the world of duality and domination. On the other hand, if we experience goals as something that are already part of us, they assist us in embracing life and moving into dominion.

What do you consider your goals? Are your goals something that exist externally, something that you need to achieve? Or do you experience your goals as something that become part of you as your energy expands?

Day 318

Revisiting Personal Freedom

I find it useful to frequently revisit how I define personal freedom. Write your definition of personal freedom today, then find your definition from the exercise of day 3. Notice whether and how your definition has evolved. If this is the first time you have written your definition, make a note to revisit it in a few months.

DAY 319

Forgiving and Being Forgiven: A Meditation

You stroll through the gardens, with their intoxicating fragrance of lavender and rose, unsure of why you are there. As you enter the temple, the air feels cool and fresh.

A woman dressed all in white motions for you to enter the sanctuary. After you bathe in scented water and dress in a soft white robe, you walk into the heart of the temple. An old man there asks for your forgiveness. You are puzzled. You don't know him and tell him there is no reason for him to make this request. He smiles and asks again. You look into his eyes and see such love you can't refuse him. As soon as you give him your forgiveness, you become filled with a peace and oneness beyond description.

As you continue to look into his eyes you see all the people in your life you have hurt. You see all the people you believe have hurt you. One by one you ask for, receive, and give forgiveness. You forgive and are forgiven. You sit down and the old man smiles lovingly and knowingly at you. You are at peace.

DAY 320

Peace of Mind

How do you know you have peace of mind? To me, that seems like an odd question. I know I have peace of mind when I have peace of mind. What brings you peace of mind? Do you have to earn it by obeying a certain set of rules or by doing some good deed, or are you simply allowed to have it? What exactly entitles you to have peace of mind?

We can have peace of mind in the midst of chaos and drama if we so choose. Become aware of the rules that govern your ability to experience peace of mind. Today give yourself permission to have peace of mind as often as possible.

DAY 321

Addictions

Fighting your addictions will only make them stronger. Embrace them fully and get clear about your choices. Then observe them but don't act upon them. Your addictions will set you free.

I "quit" smoking many times before I finally stopped. Each time I observed what helped and what didn't. The last time I did several things differently. First, I got very clear about my choices. I knew at some point I would want a cigarette. My mind would tell me I just wanted one puff, just one cigarette. I knew from experience that was a lie.

I also consciously invited my desires in. When I wanted a cigarette, instead of fighting the desire, I felt it fully. I breathed in the desire, admitted I'd kill for one puff, let it rise up, peak, and then fade back into nothingness. I embraced my desires and then chose not to act on them.

Once we embrace something, choosing how we really want to act becomes easier. Try embracing your addictions. It is much more effective than fighting them.

DAY 322

Hitting a Wall

As we explore our filter system and try to embrace our limitations there are times when it feels like we have hit a wall. No matter how hard we try, we just can't get over or around it. When my resistance to change was great, it seemed I had taken a shovel and dug a deep ditch in front of the wall, just to make sure I couldn't get over it.

When it feels like you have hit a wall in your process, have a picnic. Spread a beautiful blanket in front of your wall. Enjoy its beauty and strength, and thank it for its protection. As you sit enjoying your picnic, read the graffiti on the wall and notice its details. You'll know when you're ready to jump over it or find the door through it that has always been there. Relax, track, recapitulate, and enjoy yourself wherever you are in your process.

DAY 323

Opponents

How often do you set up the dynamic of "you against them" in your life? You against your boss, you against your judgmental thoughts, you against the system. What role do opponents play in your life? Has your filter system or your mind become an opponent? Whatever we resist persists. Embrace your opponents and treat them as welcomed guests instead. Make friends with at least one of your opponents today.

DAY 324

Ghosts from the Past: A Meditation

You are sitting at the top of a hill. The breeze feels warm and the sounds of a summer evening fill the air. You sense the love and the peace that surround you as you sit watching the stars. A shooting star delights you.

The new moon has just risen and drifts lazily across the sky. It is a time of new beginnings, but in the darkness the ghosts of the past often come back to visit us.

One by one people from your past come to join you. With some you experience joyful reunions. With others you discover a time of healing as together you release the past, forgive each other, and remember the love you once shared. These memories from the past have all come in love to help you heal. Allow the healing to occur.

DAY 325

Seeing with Clarity

Focus your attention on an object nearby. Get as close to it as you can and really focus on it. Now relax and look at it gently, with a soft gaze.

Closely focus on the object again and take a deep breath. What happens to your peripheral vision as you stare at the object?

Now look at the same object without staring. Just gaze at it softly. How do your eyes feel?

Allow your field of vision to expand until you see the object and everything around it. Look around the room and allow your focus to soften and expand until you can see the entire room. What do you see? How do you feel? Notice how your focus changes your perspective.

What is seeing with clarity? Do we ever really see clearly, or is clarity relative?

DaY 326

Dream a Little Dream

In my wildest dreams I never would have imagined having a life as wonderful as the one I am living. What are your wildest dreams? What would an ideal day feel like? Imagine waking up every morning excited about the day to come. Imagine going to bed each night feeling happy, loved, secure, and at peace.

Now allow for the possibility it can be even better. You can give yourself that gift. Just be gentle and loving with yourself and keep clearing out your filter system.

DAY 327

Shadows in the Water

Stand on the shore of a large body of water early in the morning or late in the afternoon. Make sure you can see the sun shining on the surface. If you don't live near a body of water, use a fountain or a swimming pool. Focus your attention on the shadows in the water. Breathe softly and watch the water's surface until you can feel the shadows. Return when the moon is full and do the same thing. What do you feel in the shadows? Let the shadows speak to you.

DAY 328

The Grandfather: A Meditation

You walk along the rocky path wondering where it will take you and listening to the ocean thundering in the distance. Birds soar overhead. You are lost in thought—your dream was quite clear about where to go but not why. You are so distracted that you forget to watch your step. You stumble and fall; a thin line of blood trickles down your leg. As you pull yourself up, you ask the rocks to guide your feet, reassuring them that this time you will listen.

The path descends rapidly toward the ocean. At the end of the point, an old man sits watching the sea. So this is why you are here. You approach slowly, not really sure what to say to him. He turns to look at you and all your fears fade away. His eyes sparkle in the sunlight, full of laughter, and he motions for you to sit beside him.

You sit in silence for a time; then he turns to you, and your eyes meet. You breathe deeply. He picks up a shell and holds it to your ear. The sounds of the ocean fill your being. He reaches out with his other hand and touches your heart. You feel warmth filling you with a deep knowing about the perfection of life and of the freedom love brings.

Sit beside him in peace watching the ocean, feeling your connection to everyone and everything.

DAY 329

Making a Difference

What could you do in this moment that would improve the quality of your life? Make a list of nurturing things that you can do for yourself. Include both big things and small—draw a bubble bath, get a massage. Then do at least one thing on your list every day.

DAY 330

Play

When was the last time you felt playful? Being on a spiritual path does not need to be serious—can you be playful, enjoy it, and still find the spiritual path beneficial? What if you could approach even your biggest petty tyrant playfully? What if you took today off and just played?

DAY 331

Taking Your Time

If you tend to be in a hurry or become impatient when people are slow,
practice taking your time. Go to the grocery store, have more than the
minimum number of items for the express lane, get in the express lane
anyway, and then take your time writing a check or getting your money out.
Take a really long time and notice your reaction. Make a point of looking at
the people behind you in line. Just observe, don't explain or apologize.

If you tend to take your time, notice the effect your slowness has on the
other people around you. Don't speed up; just notice.

DAY 332

The Power of the Pen

Over the years I have seen so many people resist writing even though using a pen and paper is one of the most powerful tools of transformation. Being at ease with writing is one of the best gifts you can ever give to yourself.

Get a journal today and if you do nothing else, write at least the date and a few words about how you are feeling. Do this every day until your resistance to writing not only disappears, but you come to feel the day isn't complete without at least a few minutes of writing time.

DAY 333

Releasing Energy

Pick up a rock and put everything you want to release into the rock. Then lovingly leave the rock behind.

Day 334

Being Invisible

Go for a walk in a shopping mall or park or other public place where lots of people tend to go and practice being invisible. See yourself getting smaller and smaller until you disappear. If you look at your life, you will find there are already times you have made yourself invisible—now practice doing it consciously.

DAY 335

Joy

I love to watch hummingbirds as they dart from flower to flower extracting the sweetness each flower contains.

How can you extract the sweetness of joy from your life? Today take time to savor joy. Think of something that brings you joy and do it. Go for a walk, watch a sunset, have passionate sex, or eat luscious strawberries. Fill your life with joy today.

DaY 336

Life Is a Dream

Ask yourself often throughout the day, "Am I awake or am I asleep?" Notice how you determine whether you are awake or asleep. What clues do you use? How do you know you're awake? Are you really awake or are you asleep in a dream you call life?

This exercise works several ways. Once you realize you're dreaming, you can awaken or become lucid in your dream. If you ask yourself often enough, eventually you will remember to ask yourself in your dreams, and you may induce a lucid dream. This is an opportunity for you to awaken to the dream you call life.

chapter 13

Mirror, Mirror, on the Wall

At first the girl didn't understand the reflection she saw on the surface of the water. As she looked at her own face for the first time, she realized she was pretty. Perhaps her mother was right: the other girls were jealous of her and that is why they always teased her.

She put her finger in the water and her image disappeared. In its place, she saw a rainbow-colored mist swirling round and round. Her back felt warm, her head began to spin, and she found herself being pulled into the mist. After a flutter of fear, a profound feeling of love enfolded her.

She sensed that she was everywhere and nowhere at the same time, and then a peaceful thought gently entered her mind: You are in the center of your being. You are one with your spirit. You are experiencing who and what you really are—pure, unconditional love.

She felt the presence of another and recognized it as the Grandmother. When she opened her eyes, she was once again sitting by the stream, and the Grandmother stood behind her, smiling.

"What was that?" the girl asked.

"I thought you might like to see through the eyes of love instead of fear. You see yourself as you think you are rather than how you really are. You can't see something if you don't believe it exists. You don't believe your beauty exists. You talk about your spirit, but you don't believe it is real. It is just something you think you believe in.

"Open your heart and your mind. Let yourself feel the spirit in everything about you. Feel the wisdom of the trees, the gentle caress of the wind, the soothing sound of the brook. Open your heart to nature and feel."

They sat in silence for a long time. The Grandmother filled her being with the love all around her. She looked at her young charge and smiled.

"There were two young fish who lived in the ocean. One day a lobster went by and commented, 'Isn't the water grand?'

"After the lobster swam off, one fish looked at the other and asked, 'What is water?'

"They spent the rest of their lives swimming through the oceans in search of water. Just before they died, a shark swam by, and one fish finally had the courage to ask, 'Where can we find water?'

"The shark looked at them in disbelief. As he swam off he said, 'You're swimming in it.'

"You are surrounded by spirit. It isn't something you need to find. It is something you merely need to open up and feel."

The Grandmother held the young girl's head in her lap for a long time. They sat in silence feeling the love that surrounded them.

"Love, my child. Love is the energy that will set you free. Love everything, especially your fear and your anger. Learn to look at your shadow self and love it with all your heart and all your soul. Your fear and your anger needs your love most of all. Love is the energy that can heal anything, while fear erodes your happiness."

"Whenever you come here, look into the brook and conjure up the feeling of love. Then give that love to the image you see reflected there. Keep sending your image love until you see the truth. You are a magnificent being. Learn to see yourself through the eyes of love instead of fear."

A bird sang and its joy filled the young girl's heart. She was so grateful for the presence of the Grandmother in her life.

DAY 337

The Journey

Life is a journey best enjoyed in the moment. If we are fortunate, our lives become a journey in which we connect with the essence of who and what we are. Our minds may tell us that we'll be happy once we achieve a specific goal or have a loving relationship or amass more money or attain any number of external solutions. Unfortunately tomorrow never comes. By the time tomorrow gets here, it's already today.

What is this journey called life really about for you? Is your attention so focused on achieving something that you've forgotten how to be happy in the moment? Today remember to breathe deeply and enjoy the scenery.

Day 338

Intuition

We all have intuition. It is that quiet, still voice of our spirit guiding us. Listening to our intuition makes life so much easier—if we practice listening to it about small things, it becomes easier to hear it when we think about the large things.

For years a friend and I have played "yes or no" on the phone. One of us thinks of a question with a yes or no answer. We don't share the question, we simply ask the other person to answer. At times the answers are uncanny.

Play with your intuition. Practice "guessing" and be grateful for your intuition.

DAY 339

Dropping Down

Go inside yourself and connect with your inner knowing. Doing this takes practice. You have to go through the layers of your consciousness to the core of your being. On a regular basis go inside and drop your awareness down. First you will notice your thoughts, then your emotions, and finally the feelings or sensations you have in your body. Practice dropping down until you can easily move beyond the surface and become aware of the currents deep within your being.

Start by taking a deep breath and relaxing. Take another deep breath and notice your thoughts. After you're aware of your thoughts, take a moment to notice your emotions. Allow your breath to take you a bit deeper and notice what you are feeling in your body. As you practice dropping down, you eventually will become aware of the gateway to your divinity.

Be gentle and loving with yourself as you learn to drop down and connect with your divinity.

DAY 340

Events

What events have had the most impact on your life?

Select an event that holds importance to you. How would your life be different if it had never happened? How has it affected your energy? Are you more open or more cautious since the event? How could you see the event differently? If you feel the event was "good" how could you see it as "bad" and vice versa?

DAY 341

Becoming One: A Meditation

Imagine standing in front of the expansive energy that is your Creator. Know that it is well pleased by its creation, you. You are surrounded by a sense of peace and wonder and awe. Feel the energy of creation embrace you and fill you. Breathe in the love and absolute acceptance of that energy.

Imagine becoming one with the energy of unconditional love. Feel yourself merging and surrendering your essence to love. Become one with everything. Let go of your sense of self and become one.

DAY 342

Nature of Reality

Reality is relative. What is the nature of your reality? One of the most important questions I ever answered for myself was, "Is this a hostile universe or a safe one?" The ancient Toltec seers believed that the universe was predatory and hostile and based their whole mythology on that theory. I am part of what I have come to call the new seers. My experience has been that this is a safe and loving universe. That realization has made a huge difference in my life.

The importance of this outlook on the universe has come up throughout this book. Decide for yourself now if you live in a safe or a hostile universe. You can make your universe safe by aligning yourself with your spirit. Imagine how different your world would be if you always knew you were safe and surrounded by love.

Day 343

Integration

Ultimately, any spiritual path leads to a sense of integration or wholeness. Many years ago I experienced a process called the explosion. My consciousness left my body and fragmented into millions of pieces traveling throughout the universe. One part of my consciousness went back to the beginning of time. We were all one and then in an instant we were separate entities.

When I returned, I felt an immense sadness. I felt so alone and separate. Several weeks later I revisited my experience. I realized we were all still one and that life is a process of reintegration where we separate and then come back together in that oneness.

What parts of yourself could you integrate? What parts of yourself do you judge harshly and push away? Allow yourself to lovingly move toward a greater sense of integration.

DAY 344

You Were Right, I Was Wrong, and I Am Sorry

In order to achieve personal freedom we have to break away from the stranglehold personal importance has on us. Personal importance manifests in so many ways. One of the predominant ways it shows up in our lives is in the need to be right.

In my book *The Toltec Way*, I describe a lengthy journaling process called the Book of Freedom. The process is extremely powerful. In one section, after you have cleared out substantial parts of your filter system you make a list of everyone whom you have harmed and everyone you think has harmed you. Then you contact each person and say, from your heart, "I am sorry. You were right, and I was wrong." It is incredibly freeing when you can finally do that.

There is no such thing as right and wrong. Ultimately you couldn't have harmed someone any more than they could have harmed you. Today, when the opportunity arises and you just know you are right, take a few deep breaths, go deep to the center of your being, and with as much love and honesty as you can muster, tell the person, "I'm sorry. You were right, and I was wrong." Keep practicing this until you experience just how freeing it is—especially when you just know you are right.

DAY 345

Excess

Anything, when done in excess, can be harmful. Even something as heal-ing as meditation needs to be done in moderation. Do you do anything in your life to excess? What role, if any, does excess play in your life?

DAY 346

A Flower Bud: A Meditation

The sun has just come up and a beautiful rosebud begins to gently unfold as
the sun's rays warm it. Slowly, one by one the petals uncurl. Imagine you
are that rosebud and feel yourself opening, unfurling, and allowing your
beauty to shine forth.

Imagine the rose fully open and feel the gentle touch of bees as they alight
and fly off. Feel the sun. Be one with the quiet of nature, and feel the rhythm
of life flowing through you.

Imagine the petals falling off one by one and the beautiful bud turning
into a rosehip full of the potential of new life. Now see your own life as a
beautiful bud unfolding.

DAY 347

Shifting Gears

We are beings composed of energy. When we say we are angry, a more accurate description is that we are in an energy state we have chosen to label angry. Every emotion or thought or action generates an energy state, and feeling angry refers to a certain energy configuration. Feeling safe and feeling afraid are also energy states. As you notice what those energy states feel like, you can easily learn to shift gears. If you observe that your chest is tight when you feel afraid, and open and soft when you feel safe, you can use that knowledge to shift energy states.

It is as simple as moving the muscles in your body. Your mind may be a bit more attached to holding on to your emotions, but with a bit of practice you can learn to shift energy states at will.

Practice shifting gears today. When you feel safe, generate fear. If you feel angry, generate the energy of love instead. One component of personal freedom is the ability to change energy states at will.

DAY 348

Projecting Your Consciousness

Find a small object that is visually interesting to you—perhaps a small rock, a piece of jewelry, a leaf, a flower, or even a crystal. Imagine yourself getting smaller and smaller until you can walk around on the surface. What does the object look like from this new perspective?

Imagine yourself projecting your consciousness into the object. Allow yourself to become the object. What does it feel like to be an inanimate object?

Today, practice projecting your consciousness into people, animals, and objects. It takes practice, but you can do it.

DAY 349

Have To

What does the energy of "have to" feel like? When you tell yourself you have to do something, how do you feel? How do you feel when you do something because you want to?

Is there really anything you "have to" do? We always have a choice. The results we get are influenced by our choices, but there isn't anything we really have to do. We don't even have to breathe; if we don't the consequence is death, but we don't have to do it. Our bodies choose to breathe.

What do you really have to do?

Day 350

Holding Space

Hold your hands a few inches apart and let the space between your hands fill with energy. That energy could be love, power, joy, or even fear. Fill that space with whatever kind of energy you'd like.

When I lead a ceremony, I create a place where people can connect with their divinity. I hold space. I consider holding space a sacred act. Hold space today to experience joy or freedom or whatever else you'd like to experience. Think about holding space for the people in your life, too.

DAY 351

Eating

Prepare a wonderful meal for yourself; then sit in front of a mirror and watch yourself as you dine. Eat slowly and allow yourself to fully taste each bite.

Notice any resistance you might have to doing this. As with any of the daily exercises, just do it with a sense of curiosity and no expectations.

DAY 352

Masks

What masks do you wear? What masks do you wear for your parents, your boss, your best friend, your petty tyrant? What masks do you wear when you are alone? Imagine yourself walking through your day holding your masks in front of your face. What would happen if you stopped wearing any mask at all?

Pause throughout the day and observe your mask.

Day 353

Connecting with a Loved One: A Meditation

This meditation is a wonderful method to complete unfinished business and to process unresolved emotions.

Imagine yourself standing in the mists before time. They swirl around you, embracing you. They seem to have a life of their own, and their movements mesmerize you. You feel peaceful and expansive. You know you are safe. You feel at home.

The mists begin to part and you see the loved one you thought of as dead walking toward you. His image shimmers and he smiles lovingly at you as he draws closer. You hear his voice in your heart. Take a deep breath and allow yourself to feel his presence. The love survives. Only the body dies.

DAY 354

The World in the Mirror

What do you notice when you look in a mirror? What do you say to yourself? Do you judge the image you see?

Spend some time looking at the world with a mirror. Focus through the mirror and look at a flower, or a friend, or a sunrise. What does that world you see in the mirror look like?

DaY 355

Shame

Have you ever felt ashamed of yourself, of those around you, about something someone did to you, or of any of your choices or actions? Shame is generated by judgment.

How could you view the event so you could feel acceptance instead? Today recapitulate shame and let it go.

DAY 356

The Knowable and the Unknowable

The universe is divided into the knowable and the unknowable. The ancient ones realized it was a waste of time and effort to try to know the unknowable because by definition it is unknowable.

How is your universe divided? What is unknowable to you? How much time do you spend focusing on the knowable and the unknowable? When you want to change, do you focus on your internal universe or do you try to change "out there"?

Day 357

Inside Out

Personal importance demands that we look good. Today, wear one piece of clothing inside out. When someone notices, observe how you feel but don't explain. Just look at them and say, "Yes I am." Then breathe deeply and move on about your day.

Notice if your personal importance prevents you from doing this at all or demands that you explain why if you do.

Day 358

The Void

Our sense of oneness exists just on the other side of the void. Working with the energy of the void is very powerful. The void is a place of nothingness that contains everything. The symbol of the void is a spiral.

Imagine yourself standing in front of a huge spiral. Allow it to draw you inward. What do you feel in the presence of the void? You can find your divinity in the void?

DAY 359

Wounded Animal: A Meditation

As you walk along your favorite path, you notice a small wounded animal. You speak softly as you approach. It looks longingly at you with eyes full of hope. You gently pick it up and hold it close to your heart. You stroke it lovingly and ask for guidance on how to help this being.

Place your hand over the animal and feel your hand getting warmer as the healing energy of love flows through you. You sit down, holding the animal in your lap, and begin to meditate. Close your eyes and envision the animal walking away healthy and whole again. You can feel the healing energy coming into your heart and moving through your hands. You feel love filling both of you.

After a few minutes open your eyes and discover the animal sitting in your lap, looking at you with gratitude and love. You offer up a prayer of thanks as the animal walks into the undergrowth.

Day 360

Gratitude List

Create a list of everything you are or could be grateful for. Then use that list as your mantra.

Add something to the list every day. Focus as much of your conscious awareness as you can on the feeling of gratitude. The energy of gratitude is expansive and helps us to connect with our spirit. Practice feeling this energy; let it fill your heart and your mind. Rather than thinking about it, allow yourself to feel it. Feeling and thinking are two very different activities. Practice feeling.

day 361

Pet Rock

Find a rock and make it your pet for a month. Feed it, care for it, nurture it, and ensure its happiness. Carry it with you everywhere and introduce it to your friends. Be serious about the obligation and take care of your pet rock.

Day 362

How Does Your Body Feel?

Take a deep breath and notice what you are feeling in your body. Are you rested or tired? Are you hungry or full? Does your body need exercise, fresh air, good sex, or more water? How does your body feel, and what does it need? Ask your body what it is feeling, what it needs, and then take the time to listen.

The next time you are hungry, ask your body what it wants rather than thinking about what you want. Listen to how your body feels.

Day 363

You Rule

If you were the ruler of the universe, what type of ruler would you be? What would your world look like? Whom would you invite to join you? Would there be lots of rules in your world? Would there be a supreme being? Take some time and design the world of your dreams.

What could you do to create that world in your life now?

Day 364

Wisdom

Wisdom is a product of the spirit while knowledge comes from the mind. Freedom occurs as we access wisdom and release our attachment to knowledge.

How often do you connect with your wisdom? Are you still attached to knowledge? Practice saying "I don't know" and you'll find out.

Day 365

The End

Our traditional calendar contains 365 days. If you follow nature's cycles, the moon year has only 364, and after all there really is no such thing as a year. As with so much of our life, our experience is dependent upon our perspective. So often at the end of a year we reflect, see where we have been, and spend some time thinking about where we would like to go.

How have these exercises affected your perspective? Which ones did you enjoy and which ones did you avoid?

What could you do right now to create more freedom and joy in your life?

How could you deepen your love for yourself?

Right now, in this moment choose to see your life through the eyes of love. Love even your fear. Just love and see the perfection in every moment.

afterword

The Grandmother's days were drawing to a close. She looked off to the east and called upon the spirits of the land. She called upon the ancient ones, the thunder beings, the plants, the animals, and the wind. All came to her and listened. Raising her arms to the sky, she began to chant, her melodic voice blending with the wind.

> From the ancient ones came my gifts.
> Now, they belong to all who care to listen.
> To the earth I give my wisdom.
> To the animals I give my joy.
> To the plants I give my laughter.
> To the thunder beings I give my power.
> And to the wind I give my greatest gift, the gift of my love.
> Great Spirit, hear me, help all people know their freedom.
> Help people have the wisdom and the patience to listen to
>   their hearts.
> May all who watch the sun rise with their hearts feel my
>   love.
> May all who take the time to feel the wind know your grace.
> And may all who live know themselves as spirit, pure and
>   free, made of love and light and laughter.
> Great Spirit, may all who hear these words know you.

With that the Grandmother set her consciousness free, allowing it to become one with the elements. Her love and wisdom have become a gift for anyone who will take the time to listen.

The next time you feel the wind, let it love you; let it teach you. Sit by a gentle brook and let it speak to you. Spend time with the plants and animals and let them heal you. Stand close to a tree and feel yourself becoming one with it. See the world through its eyes, feel the sap coursing through your veins. The earth holds the wisdom of all times; take the time to listen.

Go and watch a thunderstorm as it dances across the horizon. Watch the sun rise and set. Open your heart to nature and it will heal you; it will set you free. Learn how to listen. Learn to see the world as it is rather than how you think it is. Call upon the love of the Grandmother and she will reach across time to teach and to love you. Just open your heart and embrace the miracle.

a final Note

When I finish writing a book, I always feel a bit of sadness and a desire to connect with the reader personally. I wish I could sit beside you as you read these pages and answer your questions, encourage you when your fear whispers, "Stop now," or just smile and remind you that you are perfect and wonderful and brave.

My prayer for you is that you do anything necessary to enjoy life to the fullest. Use this book and its tools, listen to the quiet, still voice of your spirit, and have the courage to follow it wherever it may lead you.

If you have any questions, feel free to contact me. If you would like to connect with other like-minded individuals, I have an e-group where you can share your thoughts, ask questions, experiment, and play. I post exercises and interact as much as time permits. You'll find instructions on how to join the e-group on my Web site.

My e-mail address is sgregg@aloha.com
My Web site is *www.SusanGregg.com*

Or you can write me at:

Dr. Susan Gregg
General Delivery
Kurtistown, Hawaii 96760

(A self-addressed, stamped return envelope would be greatly appreciated.)

closing prayer

Great Spirit, gods, goddesses, all there is, my Creator, may I have the courage, wisdom, and willingness to live from love. May I always be kind and harmless to myself and to others. May I follow the path of my heart with joy and ease and gratitude. May I see only your love in the faces around me, and may the light of love shine brightly within me. May love be the beacon that gently guides me home. *Namaste*

With love,

glossary

agreements: We have all, consciously or unconsciously, made contracts or
arrangements with the people in our lives and with the world itself. We agree to
accept the beliefs of our family, friends, and society. These agreements limit our
experience of reality. We are generally unaware of them, yet they dictate most of
our choices and our actions.

assumptions: We assume that we know what another person is thinking or
feeling. We assume others think and feel the same way we do. As soon as we
make an assumption, we are dealing with our filter system and not reality.

attention: Our attention is where we choose to focus our mind, thoughts, and
actions. Whatever we focus our attention on, we get more of. If we focus on
fear, we will get more fear. If we focus on personal freedom, we will create that
as well.

awareness: Awareness dictates much of our experience of reality. It is the first of
the three Toltec masteries. Awareness is a skill we can develop. The more aware
we become of our filter system, the easier it is to release it.

beliefs: We live our lives based on our beliefs and rarely question them because we
believe them to be true. Our attachment to proving that our beliefs are true
causes most of our limitations, pain, and emotional turmoil.

ceremony: A ceremony is a sacred act of power. It can include a ritual, blessing,
prayer, or an activity. It is a wonderful way to connect with your divinity and
universal energy. Ceremonies can be very personal and transformative.
Generally they open and close with a prayer; how you fill up the space in
between is up to you.

dedication: Dedication is a deep commitment to yourself to accomplish a task. If
you dedicate yourself to achieving personal freedom, your life will be
transformed.

discipline: Discipline, when it comes from deep within, can enhance your ability to
stay focused on the task at hand, to make yourself do what you need to do, and
to follow through on your commitments to yourself.

domination: Domination is a way of looking at the world that is very linear and
based on duality. A world based on domination judges things as right or wrong,
better than or worse than, black or white. Our society is based on domination.
Domination encourages judgment, fear-based thinking, and group mentality.

dominion: Dominion is a way of looking at life that is very expansive. Symbolically it is represented by a sphere. In dominion all people are part of the great circle of life. When we live our lives based on dominion, we realize people see things differently because we all see life from a different place on the sphere. Life is as it is. From a place of dominion it is much easier to embrace our limitations and change things. Dominion encourages love and individuality.

dropping down: Dropping down is a process of going deep within your being so you can connect with your innate wisdom and goodness. It takes practice to be able to go beyond the mind chatter to the very core of your being. To drop down, breathe deeply, quiet your mind to the best of your ability, and practice going within.

emotions and feelings: Emotions are based on what we tell ourselves about reality. Angry, sad, glad, tired, happy, and upset are examples of emotions. Feelings refer to the sensations we have in our bodies, as in, "My stomach feels empty."

fault and responsibility: Fault and responsibility are too very different energy states. When we feel at fault, we feel we have done something wrong. When we feel responsible, we are merely talking about our ability to respond. Being responsible in no way means you are at fault. Make sure you don't contaminate the concept of responsibility with fault.

filter system: We see the world dimly through our filter system. It is like looking through a waterfall—our vision of the world is severely distorted. Our filter system is composed of our beliefs, agreements, and assumptions.

God: God can be an emotionally charged word for some people. For years I avoided using it in my teachings because my concept of God was so contaminated with fear and judgment. When I do use the term, I refer to the expansive, limitless energy of creation. If the word carries any emotional charge for you, consider redefining God.

intent: Intent is the third of the Toltec masteries. In the purest sense intent is the energy of creation; it is how we create our experience of reality. Learning to work with your intent is incredibly powerful and freeing.

Nagual: Nagual is the spiritual aspect of our world. It is also used to refer to a teacher who has achieved personal freedom and is guiding other people in their quest to find personal freedom.

path: The Hawaiians say there are many paths to the top of the mountain but the view from the top is the same regardless of which path you have taken. Each of us has our own unique path.

personal freedom: Each person's experience of personal freedom is unique. My definition has changed drastically over the years. It is something you define for yourself. For me, it is a deep and abiding connection to my spiritual essence.

personal importance: Personal importance is tied up with our filter system and curtails our ability to make loving choices. The more personal importance you have the less personal power you have.

personal power: Personal power is in alignment with our spirit or true self. When we make decisions from our personal power, they tend to be based in love.

power: Power is neutral. It is energy and our connection to that energy, coupled with our ability to use it.

process: A process takes time and effort. It is ongoing; most processes have a beginning, middle, and end.

seeing: I often refer to "seeing the energy." People "see" or experience the energy in a variety of ways. Some people literally see energy, some people feel it in their bodies, others hear things, and some people even taste energy. We all see in a different way; rather than judging how you do it, take the time to find out which way works best for you and celebrate it.

spiritual: Spiritual is anything that pertains to our spirit or the realm of the Nagual. We are all spiritual beings having a physical experience.

surrender: Surrender is to let go of and release our control or attachment to a person, event, or specific outcome.

tracking: Tracking is a method of viewing life that assists you in seeing your filter system. As a cat will track its prey, you can learn to track your filter system.

transformation: Transformation is the second of the Toltec masteries and refers to a large variety of tools, including tracking, recapitulation, and any tool that assists you in transforming your life.

suggested Reading

This list offers a few of my favorite books. Many of the authors listed here have also written other wonderful books, and I recommend them as well. Books seem to find us when it's time to read them, so go to your favorite bookstore and browse.

Channeled

Emmanuel's Book compiled by Pat Rodegast and Judith Stanton. Bantam Books, 1985.
Emmanuel's Book II compiled by Pat Rodegast and Judith Stanton. Bantam Books, 1989.
Emmanuel's Book III compiled by Pat Rodegast and Judith Stanton. Bantam Books, 1994.
I Come As a Brother by Bartholomew. High Mesa Press, 1986.
Reflections of an Elder Brother by Bartholomew. High Mesa Press, 1989.

Emotional Healing

Adult Children by John & Linda Friel. Health Communications, 1988.
Fire in the Soul by Joan Borysenko, Ph.D. Warner Books, 1993.
Legacy of the Heart by Wayne Muller. Fireside, 1992.

Healing

Anatomy of the Spirit by Caroline Myss, Ph.D. Harmony Books, 1996.
Back to Eden by Jethro Kloss. Back to Eden Books, 1985.
The Dragon Doesn't Live Here Anymore by Alan Cohen. Fawcett, 1993.
Earthway by Mary Summer Rain. Pocket Books, 1990.
Joy's Way by W. Brugh Joy, M.D. Jeremy P. Tarcher, 1979.
Light Emerging: The Journey of Personal Healing, by Barbara Ann Brennan. Bantam Books, 1993.
Loving What Is by Byron Katie. Harmony Books, 2002.
The Pathway by Laurel Mellin. Regan Books, 2003.
The Solution by Laurel Mellin. Regan Books, 1997.
A Touch of Hope by Dean and Rochelle Kraft. Berkley, 1999.
The Wise Earth by Janell Moon. Red Wheel, 2002.
You Can Heal Your Life by Louise L. Hay. Hay House, Inc., 1984.

Inspirational

The Alchemist by Paulo Coelho. Harper Collins, 1993.

Conversations with God Book I by G. P. Putnam's Son, 1995.
The Four Agreements by don Miguel Ruiz. Amber-Allen, 1997.
Joshua by Joseph F. Girzone. Macmillan, 1987.
The Laws of Spirit by Dan Millman. H. J. Kramer, 1995.
A Path with Heart by Jack Kornfield. Bantam Books, 1993.
Peace Is Every Step by Thich Nhat Hanh. Bantam Books, 1991.
A Return to Love by Marianne Williamson. Harper Collins, 1992.
Touching Peace by Thich Nhat Hanh. Parallax Press, 1992.
Way of the Peaceful Warrior by Dan Millman. H. J. Kramer, 1984.

Novels
The Celestine Prophecy by James Redfield. Warner Books, 1993.
Illusions by Richard Bach. DeLacorte Press/Eleanor Friede, 1977.
The Oversoul Seven Trilogy by Jane Roberts. Amber-Allen, 1995.
Tuesdays with Morrie by Mitch Albom. Doubleday, 1997.

Prosperity
Creating Money by Sanaya Roman and Duane Packer. H. J. Kramer, 1988.
The Dynamic Laws of Prosperity by Catherine Ponder. DeVorss, 1984.

Relationships
A General Theory of Love by Thomas Lewis, Fari Amini, and Richard Lannon. Random House, 2000.
Love and Awakening by John Welwood. Harper Collins, 1997.
Love is Letting Go of Fear by Gerald Jampolsky. Ten Speed Press, 1979.
Mastery of Love by don Miguel Ruiz. Amber-Allen, 1998.

Shamanism
Dance of Power by Dr. Susan Gregg. Llewellyn, 1993.
Finding the Sacred Self by Dr. Susan Gregg. Llewellyn, 1995.
Mastering Your Hidden Self by Serge Kahili King. Theosophical, 1985.
The Path of Power by Sun Bear, Wabun, & Barry Weinstock. Prentice Hall, 1987.
The Teachings of Don Carlos by Victor Sanchez. Bear & Co., 1995.
A Toltec Path by Ken Eagle Feather. Hampton Roads, 1995.
Urban Shaman by Serge Kahili King, Ph.D. Fireside, 1990.
Woman at the Edge of Two Worlds by Lynn V. Andrews. Harper Collins, 1993.

index of exercises

index of meditations

To Our Readers

Red Wheel, an imprint of Red Wheel/Weiser, publishes books on topics ranging from spunky self-help, spirituality, personal growth, and relationships to women's issues and social issues. Our mission is to publish quality books that will make a difference in people's lives—how we feel about ourselves and how we relate to one another and to the world at large. We value integrity, compassion, and receptivity, both in the books we publish and in the way we do business.

Our readers are our most important resource, and we value your input, suggestions, and ideas about what you would like to see published. Please feel free to contact us, to request our latest book catalog, or to be added to our mailing list.

Red Wheel/Weiser, LLC
P.O. Box 612
York Beach, ME 03910-0612
www.redwheelweiser.com